PENCIL ME IN

A JOURNEY IN THE FIGHT FOR GRAPHITE

JOHN T. SPENCER

SPECIAL THANKS

I would like to thank Alan Stange for all the formative feedback he offered from the first day that I began this blog. I also want to thank Russ Goerend for encouraging me to continue with the blog when it had no real story arc. A special thanks goes out to Jerrid Kruse for helping me clarify my more Luddite thoughts and provide a more balanced picture of technology criticism. There are many other dedicated readers who pushed my thinking in this process.

Thank you, also, to Dr. Strange and the EDM 310 class who left regular comments, wrote reflections in blog posts and sent e-mails to me sparking in-depth conversations. Your feedback was immensely helpful through this process.

I also want to acknowledge the work of Seymour Papert. I had no idea that he had used the metaphor of computers and pencils before I was even born. His work was truly visionary and profound. A special thank you goes out to Gary Stager for pointing me to Papert during the bizarre, viral craze of #pencilchat. Stager tirelessly works to keep Papert's works alive and relevant to a contemporary audience.

TABLE OF CONTENTS

THE STORY BEHIND THE STORY
HUMMING BIRDS AND HUMMING MACHINERY

It's a frenetic Sunday morning with blog posts, tweets and e-mails beckoning my digitized attention. Isolated in the wandering world of multi-tab interaction, I allow a tool bar to define both space and time. My sons wake up early, sometime around six.

I hold Brenna in a rocking chair while the boys play on the swings.

"Look, a hunting bird," Micah points out.

One humming bird chases the other. The other reciprocates in what feels like a game of tag. Is it war? Is it love? Is it friendly play? Is there perhaps an intersection between any of those?

Micah is silently mesmerized for perhaps twenty or thirty seconds, which is no small feat for a three-year-old. The tweets are enormous at this point - birds getting out their livelihood before it gets too hot.

It strikes me that there is more complexity in one hummingbird than in the whole lot of our humming machinery. I want to understand that complexity. Or, if it can't be understood, I want to be at peace with the mystery and the paradox of that reality.

It's easy for me to seek out a blog post on a "killer app" in the name of practicality. (Which isn't what it sounds like. You might be thinking of a pair of nun chucks that pop out of a smart phone, but that's usually not the case) If I'm not careful, I'll read a few bullet-point lists and forget that education does not occur in a cultural and social vacuum.

We are shaped by our geography; by the land, the people, the culture and the climate. We are shaped by our story – by the characters and the setting and the plot we experience. Theories emerge, not in a social or cultural vacuum, but in the layers and nuances of our narrative.

*   *   *

So, days after the hummingbird incident, I'm at the grocery store, alone with my meandering mind:

I can't believe they are playing a song from Wyclef Jean. Who would have thought his music would be grocery store fare so quickly? I guess it's not all that quick. Still, if I was an artist, it would be hard for me to think that, after all that time spent pouring over the lyrics and mixing up the vocals it is now the backdrop for people like me who are trying to decide if a dollar difference is enough to justify buying store-brand Oreos. If it were lemon juice, no problem, but these are the world's best artificial cookie product.

Okay, peanut butter. They always make such a big deal out of George Washington Carver inventing peanut butter and ignore his contributions to inventions such as the motion picture. Oh, here we go. Extra chunky? All of them are extra chunky? I don't want extra chunks, just chunks. Anyone making just plain chunky anymore? I wonder if this is sort-of peanut butter version of the way movie theaters call a small soda a large soda. Talk about Orwellian Double-Speak. I wonder when it expires. In two years? Should I even be eating anything that expires in two years? Maybe that's a good thing. Maybe all these preservatives are what keeps us alive. Perhaps we'll someday live in a planet where folks live to be two-hundred and no one needs to be embalmed.

Okay, peanut butter, apples, what else did I need? I wonder if the cashier will see this bizarre cart and think that I'm a pothead. Apples, peanut butter, ice cream, cake mix. That's normal, right? Why does that matter, John? It kind-of looks like someone with the munchies, though. Okay, reconsider that. You don't even know the cashier and you don't have much of a "pot head" look in the first place.

And so it goes, unending, meandering. I re-read the snapshot of my internal monologue and shutter. Is my mind really that shallow? Is that really the progress of civilization, that we would have true safety and leisure and spend it all wandering packaged food warehouses when we have enough to survive at home?

The lady behind me in line is chattering into her phone. "I think I need to cut back on Facebook." She talks about it as if it's a narcotic. "I just get so bored, you know." I'm not sure she's really talking to the other person so much as talking to herself. I get the sense that she's not very comfortable with a meandering mind. Perhaps she's scared that she'll find herself boring or as shallow as my internal monologue.

I want to write about this, but should I just tweet it out instead? Or should I blog?

Social media.

If it's a social version of media, then it's better than watching small claims court judges berate people on daytime television. But if it's a media version of social interaction, it's a little more perplexing. I yearn for a front porch and neighbors I know on a deep level. Christy does this naturally just about every day. The truth is that sometimes I like to hide on a couch, reading a book. I

THE STORY BEHIND THE STORY

can get pretty anti-social, media or not. Maybe it is a drug.

It hits me that I'm not too different from the cell phone loud talkers. I can get pretty uncomfortable with the silence. I now have a strange kinship with Smart Phone Loud Talker. I tweet when I feel lonely. I tweet to hear my own voice when I'm afraid my words don't matter. Maybe it is a drug.

Ultimately that's what it's all about. That's why I choose to tell stories, because it is never as simple as a list of new applications. I want to tell a human story about technology, because I want to make sense out of my own identity within my own technocratic context.

*   *   *

I began the blog *Adventures in Pencil Integration* as an attempt to think through my own narrative in educational technology. I chose the nineteenth century because it removes me from the constant need for the cutting edge. It's also an easy fit, because I'm wired for metaphor. Wired? Sadly I chose a tech metaphor to describe my core identity and on some level, it's an accurate metaphor. I am shaped by the wired world. Except when I'm barefoot in the backyard watching a hummingbird. Then I'm connected right as I become disconnected.

I chose fiction, because I had the freedom to tell the truth by not telling the truth. I had the chance to describe things honestly without worrying that I had told someone else's story or that I was attacking some current trend. The last thing I wanted was to send the message that I hated a specific tribe of techies. I almost gave up several times, because there isn't a solid story arc. But then again, my own journey hasn't fit well within a story arc. It's been much closer to a postmodern narrative where the twists are found in the subtleties of life and nothing is quite what it first appears.

CHAPTER ONE
It's Not Opium and It Won't Kill You

I must have been ten years old when I bought my first pencil and held it in my clunky hands. For the first time, I could sketch a world of gray, lacking permanence and open to change. It was a medium that fit my life; leaving the red rock west for the flat agrarian haven of Kansas and into the industrial smokestacks of this city.

Gray.

Movement.

True, I played tag and leap frog in the streets. But when the world felt too compressed, I would crawl into the fire escape and open a crisp blank sheet. I would begin subtly, with tentative lines and the occasional bold stroke. I would hear the mockery from below. They called me "Graphite Geek" and "Pencil Pusher." I

CHAPTER ONE

suppose our neighborhood had a special affinity for all things alliterated.

Still, I would shade in the lines, blending carefully with the tips of my fingers. For some, the smell of grass creates a sense of nostalgia. However, I experience a flood of memories whenever my thumb accidentally brushes up against the rough edges of a freshly sharpened pencil.

Mostly I drew fantastical creatures, with dragons and sorcerers and wood gnomes. The pictures always took place in the edgy Colorado cliffs of my early childhood or in the flatlands of my midwestern memory. The pencil seemed to expand my world while allowing me the freedom to mourn the loss of space forged by the factory.

In high school, I would pull out my well-worn journal and sketch out a world of words, bound only by iambic pentameter. I would carefully erase a line of verse until it felt finished. Except it never was. For all the talk of mastery, the pencil would silently remind me, "there's always a chance for change. Nothing is permanent, kid." The modern age, I suppose.

The pencil became my refuge and the solitary fire escape my place to think through life. I guess that's what I'm hoping for right now. I want to build a Pencil Palace in my classroom context. In our factory-built urban environment, I want students to experience the freedom of pencils.

*   *   *

I have this vision of a twentieth century classroom with a pencil for every student. It goes beyond simply a few new pencils.

PENCIL ME IN

I picture telegraphs and phonographs and mimeographs and pretty much anything with the suffix -graph that my mind can conjure up. The students are excitedly learning relevant skills that they'll need for the new industrial economy. I exist, not as the expert, but as a guide, gently moving forward, offering something relevant to my students.

It is for this reason that I attend the PIE (Pencil Integrated Education) Conference in the summer of 1897. Educators are quite fond of acronyms, but this year it feels a bit awkward. See, a whole sleuth of culinary enthusiasts arrive on a train only to realize that our conference is more about learning with paper than cooking with crust. Since they can't get a refund or a one-way ticket back, they make the best of it.

Paul the Preindustrial Poet pulls me aside, "Hey Tom, you should check this out. Have you ever heard of this?"

A few of the pie enthusiasts follow us as we amble toward a booth where a man is advertising a new organizational structure for classrooms.

"What is this?" I ask.

"This is Chalkboard. It's a course management system. You get it all in one package. We will ship you a few boxes and you'll get a binder for every student, a grade book for yourself and several folders for storing student work," he says.

"I'm impressed," I tell him.

Paul holds the binder, "Look at this. There's a built-in calendar so that students can write their assignments and keep track of grades. They even have tabs with all the categories chosen ahead of time. Seriously, this is genius, Tom. You should get your district to buy these if you're going to get that one-to-one pencil to student ratio next year."

It becomes immediately awkward, with the unspoken recognition that as a "black" man in a "black" school, his students won't have access to fancy new systems.

"I know. I would just collect all the binders and record the grades in the grade book when I'm done. It would be so easy," I point out.

A woman walks up and begins perusing the binder. "I'm not really a teacher. I'm a pie enthusiast."

"Well, pie is pretty special," I point out.

"Indeed. But, I couldn't help but notice your excitement over this. It's a binder. What's so special about that?" she asks.

"Are you serious? It's a whole organizational system," I respond.

"Yes, but are you already organized as a teacher?" she asks.

"Sure, but this takes care of the organization for me," I respond.

She looks perplexed and hesitates before continuing, "Wouldn't it make more sense to develop something a little more specialized for your own needs? You know, if someone tried to organize my recipe cards for me, I'd get angry. I very well might whack them over the head with a rolling pin," she says.

Her friend adds, "Besides, don't you want students to learn how to organize information on their own?"

"I suppose, but this is more efficient," I respond.

PENCIL ME IN

"Don't confuse efficiency for effectiveness. Why not just tell kids to organize their work according to their own needs? It could be a folder or a binder or a back pocket for all I care. Aren't you more concerned with learning than with organizing assignments?" she asks.

The vendor grows visibly irritated, but I'm beginning to think the pie lady is onto something. I walk away without grabbing a pamphlet.

While I've managed to avoid the snake oil solutions of new binders, it's harder not to grow glossy eyed during the conference workshops. As the keynote speakers bust out the PowerSlides on the Edison projector, I daydream of the crisp new pencils that students will grip with joy. I'm buying into the promise of instant results for a moderate price.

It's harder still to avoid the more subtle sales pitch – that of a Utopian worldview. When I'm at a workshop and a presenter shares a story of gaining access to pencils, I find myself scribbling notes in hope that *his* story will lead to *my* success. I start thinking that it might just be a miracle drug that can save my students from the banality of a nineteenth century education. So, I leave the conference with a certain zeal that I've never experienced before. I'm going to change the world, one pencil at a time. I'm going to be the soldier in the fight for graphite.

*   *   *

Eventually, the optimistic high begins to fade as I step onto the drab gray industrial center of my neighborhood. I avoid the hype of the conference and focus on the simple task of a pencil-based

CHAPTER ONE

education. I meet with members of the community who agree to donate used pencils.

A local shop owner tells me, "It's not much. I can send you half-used pencils each week. I'll deliver them straight to your classroom if you'd like me to."

"I appreciate that," I tell him. I try to stay subtle, but I'm near giddy. I'm twelve again, sitting on the fire escape, sketching out my escape in shades of gray.

He adds, "I think it's a tragedy that we don't have a one-to-one ratio. This is the future. This is what will save education. I'm not referring to myself here. My pencils aren't great, but if everyone in the community could contribute, imagine that!"

We end up talking pencils for about an hour, swapping stories of our sketches and marveling over a world that allows for erasures of mistakes.

*   *   *

A week later, I'm in my classroom examining our pencils. Some are worn nearly to the nub. Many lack erasers. It's a hodgepodge mix of traditional wood and shiny yellow Eberhards. The paper isn't fancy, but it's free. I talk to Linus, a paper mill volunteer who promises to provide free paper out of his desire for open access to resources.

I carry boxes of fresh supplies to my new classroom. It's my second year of teaching, but my first year in this school. A veteran teacher, Mr. Brown, pulls me aside to share his thoughts on this new endeavor, "Could I see you, Techno-Tommy? I want to talk about your one pencil for every student ratio."

PENCIL ME IN

"Pretty exciting, huh?" I say, stroking the wax on my handlebar mustache.

"Well, that's the issue. I just don't see it as being the best option for our students. After all, this is about the kids," he adds.

"What do you mean?" I ask.

"It's an academic issue, really. I just don't think we need to spend class time teaching pencil skills," he says.

"Neither do I. That's why we'll embed the paper and pencil into the curriculum," I explain.

"Yes, but they've been using slates and chalk. They'll be ages behind."

"Okay, but they'll catch up quickly. They're pencil natives. They get this stuff practically out of the womb," I tell him.

"Perhaps, but the high-stakes exams are taken in ink or with a slate and chalk. How will they ever reach William McKinley's Caravan to the Top using paper and pencil?" he asks.

"But paper and pencil is what they'll use in life," I say.

"Yes, but the United Kingdom is expanding across the world and we cannot compete in an imperialist global economy if our students lag behind because we are focusing our time on paper and pencils."

"So, it's all about winning a global pissing contest?" I ask.

He stares at me blankly. "I'm sorry. These are Victorian times and I don't think it's necessary to use such vulgar language."

"Sorry. I just . . . I think pencils just might be the solution," I tell him.

"Have you watched the students with pencils? I mean really

watched them outside of school? They make spit balls and pass notes. I think it's a medium designed for amusement. It's educational opium in my opinion," he explains.

"Do you really think pencils will be that distracting?" I ask.

"I do. I think it's a step backward," he says firmly.

"We'll see."

"Yeah, we'll see alright. We'll you your opium den," he whispers to himself as he leaves.

*   *   *

Later that day, we go to our professional development meeting. Our new principal institutes a norm regarding the use of paper and pencil in professional development meetings.

"I'm not angry with anyone, but I did notice some grids of Buzzword Bingo and several people who were passing notes or drawing pictures instead of using their paper for note-taking. To avoid the distractions, we will add this to our collective norms."

I feel split on this issue. On one hand, I agree with him. Members of our staff are not truly present when their head is in a notebook. Often, the note passing becomes a distraction and they miss crucial information. And I understand why Buzzword Bingo would feel disrespectful to a presenter.

However, I see this as a bandage on a festering open wound. Teachers are not actively engaged in professional development, because the meetings are not engaging. If I sit silently without a paper in my hand, my mind will wander. And, while the system would love to take that as well, as long as I have self-determination, I have my own mind.

PENCIL ME IN

People in power seem scared of pencils, viewing them as the drug that will take students away from learning. There is hysteria about the medium, perhaps because it feels so uncertain compared to ink and too permanent compared to a slate. On some level, I get it. But if it is a drug, wouldn't it be better to learn what sickness the drug cures rather than banning it altogether?

A better solution would be to change professional development so that:

- It is relevant so that teachers feel that what they are doing connects to the subject they are teaching
- It is collaborative and horizontal so that teachers can provide their own expertise
- It is assessed on a student or school-wide level
- It is interactive
- It takes into consideration issues of self-efficacy and motivation and not simply skills. Yes, it's cool to know a skill, but what about the conceptual knowledge and the notion of how a skill will be used in the classroom?
- It models how we would want to teach. In other words, don't lecture to me about the vices of lecturing to students.
- It is pencil-integrated. Yes, allow teachers to use our binders and paper and pencil in graphing data, writing up proposals and creating lessons together. Let them write reflections in journals.

Instead of banning binders, I would use them in a pencil-based approach to professional development. If you make it interesting, you might find that I won't be sketching cartoons making fun of former president Grover Cleveland.

It has me wondering if the same fear of pencils that my principal exhibits is also the same fear that drives pencil segregation. People are scared of a different style of teaching. As a tool, pencils suggest a loss of control, an embrace of change and a resistance to the irrelevant.

*   *   *

As I visit the staff lounge, I hear a group of teachers whining about the pencil. They say it will make kids shallow. They say shorthand language is ruining academic prose (as if students completely lack the ability to shift registers. Don't they move from slang to academic language in oral speech?) They say that pen pal networks are America's newest drugs.

"It's true. Kids these days are addicted to pen pal networks. I read about it in a paper," a teacher explains.

"I suppose speech is addicting, too. And water. It's like I can't live without it. Water, that is. Non-stop. When I get up in the morning, I think to myself, 'I need water.' Am I addicted to that as well?"

"It's not the same thing at all," a teacher tells me.

"A medium is a medium," I explain.

"If it's just a medium, why do you love it so much?" Mrs. Jackson asks.

I'm stunned. I have no way to defend myself but I'm not about to back down this easily.

"I love what it can do," I tell her.

I think about the pencil conference and the techo-buzz we all felt. Perhaps it is a drug. Perhaps more dangerous than I first thought. For all my mockery of professional development, I wonder if it's not a symptom of a dwindling attention span forged by the telegraph. I think about my long conversation with the shop owner and my interaction with Mr. Brown. We talked like addicts, but the drug wasn't the pencil. It was a dream, an ideology that pencils can bring perfection.

I have to remind myself that a pencil cannot be the miracle drug that brings peace to our "globalized, graphite society." Unlike the shop owner or the conference speakers, I shouldn't see the tool as evidence of social progress.

However, I don't think we are raising a generation of stupid, illiterate, shallow thinkers and paper addicts, either. I see potential in the portability of knowledge, in the ability to erase and in the ability to edit information so easily. I see the pencil as a part of a larger trend of recording, compressing and sharing information instantaneously. This will be the generation that erased geography with trains and horseless carriages and spoke across the world with a telegraph.

So I'm left with this gray middle zone, confused by the reality that pencils can be really powerful both for progress and for regress. I'm struck by the sense that I don't have a clue what I'm doing. Like the medium itself, I'm realizing that this will be a sketchy, confusing journey with many erasures and very few well-worn lines.

Nothing is written in ink.

CHAPTER TWO
PENCIL NATIVES AREN'T ALWAYS PENCIL CITIZENS

It's no secret that the Panic of 1896 has really taken a toll on tax revenues. While robber barons created a Wall Street oligopoly leading to our economic collapse, somehow it is public education that faces the huge pay cuts. I'm not surprised, then, when I open a letter with an explanation that, while my students will have pencils and paper next year, we will not have any device for storage.

My wife Ruth is outraged. "What are they going to do, put the pencils in a pocket? That will puncture a scrotum."

"I guarantee that parents will not let their children take pencils home. Pencils will snap. Paper will be crinkled. Then there is the issue of potential stabbing. This may very well ruin the entire initiative," I lament.

"Can't they just put the pencil in a different kind of box? You talk about the fact that your students are Pencil Natives. Doesn't a native know how to carry tools? It seems to be the most rudimentary skill," she points out.

"The district won't allow it. The only accepted protocol is a pencil box," I explain.

"Why is that?" she asks.

"They say that it has to do with weight distribution. It's science, pure science, as infallible as using leeches or practicing phrenology."

"Okay, so think about my citizenship idea. Why not turn this into a conversation about who owns the pencils, what is common property and how to be stewards of what they own collectively? This can be a time to teach responsibility through dialog rather than punishments and rewards. Really, does the district own the pencils if private citizens donated them?"

"I'm going with that. The school always harps on democratic thinking and citizenship. This is a perfect chance. What more could our society need for a thriving democracy than students who think critically?"

"They could allow women to vote," she adds with a smirk.

*   *   *

So in the first week of school, I show the students the pencils. Instead of providing a long list of rules, I ask what it means to be stewards of pencils.

"It means we take care of them," a student responds.

"It's more than taking care of them. It means we use them wisely. Just making sure we don't snap pencils isn't enough," a boy adds.

"I think it means remembering where it comes from," a student answers. "I sometimes forget that my education comes at the cost of losing a forest. It's pretty humbling when you think of it that way."

"Who owns these pencils?" I ask.

"Didn't you say you had them donated?" a student responds.

"Yup, every one of them," I tell the class.

"So, do they belong to the school or do they belong to the public or do they belong just to the classroom?" a student asks.

This leads to a discussion about public and private property, about when it is okay to break the rules and about whether taking home pencils truly violates a district mandate.

"If there is no law and it's outside the law, is it illegal?"

I leave it up to the students to decide. Some students bring their own pencils from home. (Which I've cleverly termed BYOP) Some students take the pencils home while others believe that the ethical thing would be to treat them as school property and wait to see if we get pencil cases. I start to think that maybe we underestimate the citizenship capabilities of Pencil Natives. Perhaps moving into a twentieth century pedagogy will be easier than I had imagined.

*　　*　　*

A week later I'm in the midst of a discussion with a parent about the concept of a new, paper pedagogy. I assure her that most of the students will not stab one another if a teacher is doing a decent job with classroom management.

PENCIL ME IN

From across the hall, Gertrude the Cognitive Achievement for Nuanced Data-driven Year-round Learning Acquisition New Development (CANDY LAND) Specialist cuts in, "I'm worried about the classroom management issues. I mean, what happens if kids choose to pass notes instead of paying attention?"

"If learning is meaningful, you'll find that . . . " I begin.

"But a teacher can't compete with drawing pictures. Kids will want to draw pictures. At least with a slate, one can check their hands to see if they erased a picture."

Mrs. Jackson adds her concerns, "Besides, what would happen if they break a pencil. I heard that in some places kids actually snap pencils in half and throw them. I'm concerned about student safety in some classrooms. Imagine the projectiles!"

"Plus," adds Mr. Brown, "you want to allow students to use paper and pencil at home. What if they send a letter to a pedophile pretending to be a pen pal? You can't do that with a slate, can you?"

"So, you teach them pencil citizenship," I respond. "

Gertrude shakes her head, but I continue, "If they don't get it here, where will they get it? They'll go underground with their pencils rather than learning to be responsible. We have to start empowering students now."

I tell them the story of my students' conversation and they nod politely while still insisting that pencils are simply too dangerous for a classroom.

*   *   *

Apparently, there are new, ultra-portable mechanical pencils that don't require a sharpener. I had never heard of that until my students introduced me to the new tools, but my God, the ingenious methods of industrialization! Will the progress ever stop? We very well might be at the pinnacle of technological development as a society.

Should students be able to bring mechanical pencils into a pencil-integrated classroom? Can we handle the diversity of both various paper types and pencil types? Should we have a uniform set of learning tools or should we allow for customization based upon personality and preference?

I wrestle with the potential equity issues now the tools are truly different from one student to the next. So, I bring this topic up to Mrs. Jackson, the Language Arts (which incidentally is less about the art of language as much as the science of grammar and syntax) department chair (which incidentally does not have anything to do with chairs, but is more about managing a committee).

"I think we should let kids bring in whatever pencils they want," I explain.

"But won't that be unfair to students? What if one student comes to school with a fancy glittery pencil that shines when the light hits it? You know what I'm talking about, right?"

"Uh huh, go on," I motion to her.

"So, you supply your students with those bland yellow pencils. It just doesn't seem equitable," she complains.

"I see your point. However, students come to school with different clothes and with different books and no one is complaining about that. Yes, I'd love for every student to have something fancy. However, it's not about the glitz. It's about learning," I explain.

Mr. Brown cuts in, "I'm not trying to tell you how to teach, but have you considered that it will be chaotic and disorganized? How are you supposed to problem-solve when you have multiple pencil types? You'll have one kid asking for help in sharpening his pencil while another student asks you to help her refill her mechanical pencil. I couldn't do that, but maybe you could pull it off."

"Why don't we teach kids to problem-solve their pencil issues? I have a hunch they have been doing some of that on their own at home. Let's be real, none of us knew about the mechanical pencils until students brought them in." (I use that term "let's be real" far too often. It's not as if I had been talking about wood gnomes and dragons and unicorns)

It seems that the greatest barrier to pencil-based learning is not the students' lack of knowledge, but the teachers' lack of trust. Instead of being humble and learning from the students, we're seeing their knowledge as a threat to our authority. We're missing out on a chance to help Pencil Natives become better citizens, because we're scared.

*　　　*　　　*

I'm at a smoky bar sipping a watered-down pint. Factory workers shuffle in, exhausted from fourteen-hour shifts. They're covered in soot and they smell of phosphates. As they order a pint, I am torn between guilt for my labor-free job and the sense that a twentieth century education might free my students from this type of life.

CHAPTER TWO

Still, a new pedagogy can't occur when teachers are terrified of pencils. I vent about all of this to Paul the Preindustrial Poet. "Look, Tom, you have to see the bigger picture."

"I do see the whole picture. They're jealous because my students are enjoying pencil-based lessons."

"Maybe. But you also have to realize that they see you come in as this new teacher with some revolutionary teaching device and they seem skeptical."

"Skepticism? It seems more like fear," I tell him.

"Perhaps. But they've seen so many things that are supposed to be the savior of education. New programs and ideas and whatnot. They are rightfully skeptical. So when you think you are defending yourself, you're probably alienating them more than you think."

"Pencils shouldn't even be an option. If it's a good tool, use it," I begin."

"Good teachers will eventually gravitate toward good tools. But the real issue is relational. Give them a chance," he responds.

I shake my head vehemently. I'm not about to compromise with the enemy. I've worked too hard to push pencil integration thus far.

He takes a long sip from his pint, "So, you're an expert on pencils. I mean, you didn't know about the mechanical ones, but you listened and so you learned."

"True," I say.

"Well if you can listen to students why not listen to your colleagues? They both have areas of expertise, I assume. I've seen

PENCIL ME IN

Mrs. Jackson teach. She's amazing. When was the last time you asked her for advice?"

I shrug my shoulders.

"Think about it this way: what makes a pencil so powerful?" he asks.

"It can erase. It can create shades of gray. It's dynamic."

"So, if those are really the virtues of a pencil, why are you stamping these relationships with your colleagues in ink?"

*   *   *

So, I give it a shot. Once we begin to drop the whole Alpha Male thing, Mr. Brown and I are able to be a little more honest and open. I start asking more questions and realize that Mr. Brown isn't abrasive so much as unfiltered. He's a hefeweizen and I had assumed he was simply a bitter IPA.

Toward the end of the first quarter he visits my classroom and says, "You know Techno-Tommy, I may have been too harsh in my criticism of pencils. It seems that the two different pencil platforms aren't really getting into the way of learning. I mean, I saw what they did in writing their autobiographies. I like the mix of the sketches and the writing and the poetry. Very modern."

"Thanks Mr. Brown," I respond.

"I know that our students are smart. I know that they are capable of understanding something as complex as a pencil. I guess I filtered it through my own experiences as a clumsy eighth grader. I could hardly remember to wipe my slate clean after every problem."

"Yeah, I get what you're saying. I guess we all do that."

CHAPTER TWO

Later that day, when we start new unit, I explain to the students that they will need to create some documents. I assume the skills will transfer over from the students' use of Pen Pal networks and pencil logs (which I like to call plogs).

"Here's how it works. When you are done with your document, write your name at the top and then save it inside of your folder," I explain.

Pretty simple, right? Students of the Pencil Native generation should understand this without my explicit directions. After all, they've been raised around these tools. However, I am surprised the next day when students can't find their documents.

One girl says, "I set it in a folder and wrote the name on the folder."

"Did it already have a name on the folder?" I ask.

"Yeah, but I thought it was like a slate, where we change names when we change slates," she answers.

Not a problem. I pull papers out and pass them out, but I quickly run into a stack of nine papers that are untitled. Two students have no papers at all.

"Where did you put yours?" I ask one boy.

"I left it on the desk top," he responds.

"Then it was probably put in the trash," I explain.

"Uh oh," a boy interrupts. "So that metal bin is a trash can?"

"Why?" I ask.

"I put my document in there," he laments.

"Didn't you read the word 'trash can' on the side?"

He shakes his head sheepishly. "I mean, I can get it back, can't

I?"

"The custodian emptied the trash yesterday. What did you expect?" I ask.

"At home we only empty the trash once a week. I had no idea I would lose it like that," he complains.

The boy next to him explains, "I erased it. I forgot that it wasn't like a slate. I forgot that you have to save it."

Mrs. Jackson enters the room in the midst of the chaos. I turn to her and say, "I'm done. I'm done with papers and pencils and folders and kids setting papers in the trash. I'm done with pencil sharpeners that leave dust on the ground and . . . "

She explains, "I'm not a fan of pencils. You know that. However, where else are they going to learn some of these basics? Yes, students are advanced, but they miss some of these small skills about organizing their papers or writing their names or setting them in folders. I don't recommend wasting class time teaching this, but if they learn some of these pencils skills, then isn't that just a bonus of a meaningful education?"

"I guess that's true," I admit.

I think back to the PIE Conference I attended in the summer. The presenters spoke eloquently about each medium and how students would use it for amazing projects. While I do not deny the power of pencils, there was an element missing from the discussion. No one seemed to recognize the developmental level of eighth graders. No one reminded me that kids will do some illogical, confusing things simply because they are kids.

Mrs. Jackson leaves the room with this reminder, "If pencil

literacy is like true literacy, you need to give your students permission to make big mistakes. My grandson is four and barely recognizes letters. A few times he's even torn a page or two out of a book. But my hope is that he'll eventually grow into a love of reading."

It leaves me wondering if maybe I'm wrong about Mrs. Jackson as well. In a moment of weakness, I admitted that I was . . . weak. However, instead of clobbering me, she was kind. Maybe there's power in vulnerability.

*   *   *

In the next unit, I allow students to engage in pencil-based research. I assume kids will understand how to look at the bias of a source, figure out the facts and summarize the information. Instead, I watch a disturbing trend emerge.

Students pull out their note cards and begin writing everything they read. Everything. Apparently "research" means, "become a medieval scribe."

I pull the group together and say, "If I wanted copies, I'd be running a printing press." Students stare at me blankly, missing the sarcasm.

"You should do that," a student says. "You love to read and write. It would be a good summer job." Yep, they're literalists.

It's not their fault. I had assumed that their prior experience with pencils would automatically mean they could think critically about information. However, it turns out that mastering Hang Man does little to prepare a student for such thinking.

The next day the trend continues, but this time a few students pull out scissors and simply copy and paste from the *Encyclopedia Britannica.*

On some level, I don't mind. The British already have a monopoly on trade and language and imperial domination. Do they really need to be the experts on all of humanity's collective knowledge? Still, we have books with gaping holes, because students simply stole information without even bothering to copy it into their own words. So now the librarian now hates me. It doesn't help that she and Gertrude are close friends.

The next day I begin, not with the notion of research, but with the concept of intellectual property. Here, I separate the class into groups of four and have each group solve a complex, creative problem. I then allow two spies to steal an idea and use it in their group. I do a similar thing with a short paper students write.

When the students begin to complain, we have a class discussion on collaboration versus intellectual property theft. We discuss the need to share information and make it one's own rather than simply copy the work of others.

I provide them with two options. Either they can use a chart or they can use note cards. However, for each source, they must include the following:

- a question they are trying to answer
- facts (in their own words)
- bias of the source (with at least one loaded word)
- a citing of the source

Students don't plagiarize much anymore, but it required some modeling. For all the talk of the Pencil Generation and Pencil

CHAPTER TWO

Natives and the telegraph promising to instantly connect information from around the world, my students still need help learning to decipher what is true and how to articulate their own argument based upon research. In other words, they might be natives, but they still need to learn how to master the native language.

*   *   *

When the quarter closes, Paul the Pre-Industrial Poet and his wife Gloria invite us over for dinner. I take a copy of the Acceptable Use Agreement with me so that I can grill Paul on his approach to pencil citizenship.

"Paul, do your students sign a Acceptable Use Agreement?"

"They do. I pass it out on the first day."

I hand him mine and ask him for his thoughts. "I don't like it much, I admit. It's not like we have a Acceptable Use agreement for math class. Yet, we hand out protractors that can quickly turn into shanks."

My wife adds, "What about Language Arts? Why isn't there an Acceptable Use Agreement on the dangerous dark art of words? Last time I checked, nations still go to war over words."

I turn to Paul and ask him why he bothers with it.

"Look, I'm not against the Acceptable Use Agreement, per se. I'd love to have an Acceptable Use Philosophy that covers all classes. Don't we want kids to use the resources effectively?"

It has me thinking that maybe we have it all wrong with our concept of pencil citizenship. Yes, there are creepy perverts on the pen pal networks. Yes, kids can stab one another with pencils. But the real danger is in a culture of temporary and instant knowledge. True citizenship means thinking critically about bias and propaganda and learning the basic life skills to thrive in a modern world. Perhaps we need to go from "acceptable" to "ethical" and from "safe" to "free."

The Pencil Native Story

Once upon a time, there was a group of pencil pioneers who pushed their way into the Slate Land and conquered it in the name of education. All was well for the Pencil People, who changed the name from Slate Land to the rather uncreative Pencil Land. In fact, they grew rather giddy over the prospects of raising Pencil Natives in this brave new world they had created.

So, they decided it wasn't important to show a kid how to use an eraser or use blending and shading. In fact, it wouldn't be important that they learned how to write at all, because being a native automatically made one a perfect citizen immersed in the culture.

The Pencil Natives wandered aimlessly, never knowing how to use the tools of their own culture. Some teachers pointed this out and wondered if these children had actually been born in Pencil Land at all. They missed the reality that the Pencil Natives were comfortable with pencils and had, indeed, internalized the value system of a Graphite Globe. They were creating a world that was ambiguous, confusing, and gray. They were erasing any remnants of history and replacing it with every-changing, bite-sized information.

Others said that the old folks were simply clueless and that they should delight in the fact that the Pencil Natives spent their days making paper gliders and paper balls and playing Hang Man instead of writing poetry. After all, this was their world and we should learn from them. We should let them be our mentors and tutors and guides, because they knew more about pencils than the Pioneer Generation.

The two sized polarized the issue into a binary reality that missed the nuances of the argument. Instead of asking, "How do we help Pencils Natives make sense out of a graphite globe?" or "How do we get Natives to criticize the tools they use and use the tools they criticize?" they focused on the question of, "Why aren't they getting it without our help?" Instead of asking, "What does citizenship mean and how can pencils be used to sharpen critical thinking?" the adults obsessed for hours about whether or not pencils were luring in creepy outsiders.

So, the Pencil Natives grew up with the dual reputations of Saviors of the Graphite Globe and Dumbest Generation Ever and all the while they secretly yearned just to be kids with pencils, trying to make sense out of their world and their place within it.

CHAPTER THREE
Your Chart Isn't Smart

My principal walks into my classroom on a teacher workday and says, "Tom, we have a consultant here who works for Pencil Island."

"Is he really a consultant or a salesman?" I ask.

"Just meet with him. He tried sending you a telegram and you never answered," he says sternly.

Busted.

"Sorry, I meant to go see him. My horse was sick. I'll . . . I'll meet with him I guess."

Minutes later, I'm ushered into a room where a smiling man greets me with a plastic grin and a firm handshake. "I brought you some bagels and Coke. I hope you don't mind."

"I'm not sure I should be consuming cocaine, but I'll have a

CHAPTER THREE

bagel." It's strikes me that the Coca-Cola and the product he's selling aren't entirely different: sweet, efficient, addicting, but in the end deadly to a child.

"We have a whole system that you can use in a pencil-based classroom. Imagine this: each child learns discreet skills independently. Step-by-step they move through a sequential order designed for the mastery of each math, reading and writing skill. It is powerful. Indeed, it pretty much replaces the role of the teacher. As we think of a modern pedagogy and differentiated instruction, you need resources to reach every child, every time," he explains.

If only I had my Buzzword Bingo card with me. I probably wouldn't have a blackout, but definitely a five-in-a-row.

"Wouldn't it make sense to have students use paper and pencil to write essays and solve equations? What if they did some of it independently and worked cooperatively together instead?" I argue.

The slick suit snake oil salesman answers, "That sounds great. But aren't you tired of kids not working? This allows each child to work at his or her level independently. Each time they do a worksheet correctly, you put a stamp on the paper. If they pass all the pencil-based worksheet tests, they can earn the chance to play a pencil game. You can even allow free drawing time if you'd like. Games, drawings, it has it all."

"Doesn't this send the message that reading is a boring chore that requires a reward?" I ask.

"The students already find it boring because they can't read. Wouldn't you find teaching boring if you didn't know how to teach?" he asks.

PENCIL ME IN

"If I didn't know how to teach I would use this product instead," I answer.

"Exactly. The program is designed to fit the needs of teachers struggling to provide adequate intervention." Intervention? Are we dealing with drug addicts here or with children who can't comprehend expository text?

"I just don't see the appeal of this. It's a series of worksheets," I explain.

"Wrong! It's an academy. It's a whole system of learning. Kids get to pick their worksheets and the follow the instructions. Can you help every kid at every moment?"

"Well, I can't. But if I have given them the freedom . . ."

"So, you can't? Is that correct?" he asks.

"No, but . . ."

"There you have it," he points to the principal. And so, with that, the con artist and his con academy have prevailed over the voice of a teacher.

The principal cuts in, "Do teachers need training on this?"

"We provide our own professional development. However, trust me, it's a very user-friendly system. Teachers love it, because it replaces the teacher with the program. Think of it this way. You move from a sage on stage to a guide on the side."

Note to self: never trust someone who answers in rhymes.

Don't get me wrong. There is a time to practice discreet skills. However, if you aim for "basic skills" you won't hit it. If students work on authentic pencil-integrated projects, though, and have to use critical thinking, the skills will increase along the way.

CHAPTER THREE

"You should consider this program. It's a whole system of worksheets."

Therein lies the problem. Find the root word. Work. It's a factory model based upon an industrial metaphor.

And yet . . .

I often require my students to work, not based upon their own inquiry, but based upon what I think is best. My approach is still top-down, with little room for student input. For all my talk of a new Twentieth Century pedagogy, this meeting leaves me feeling uneasy. If this is progress, I'm not ready to move forward.

*   *   *

Later in the quarter the principal pulls me aside and says, "Hey Techno-Tommy, we have this new aid who will be going to your class. He's an excellent resource. His name is Ed Helper. Nice guy. You'll enjoy working with him."

I don't doubt that he makes my job easier. For a half hour, he passes out various worksheets (emphasis on the word "work" rather than "learn"). The students do not particularly like him, despite his generally peppy demeanor.

I just don't think the students are learning from his guidance. Sure, they read a worksheet and yes, they use a pencil. But it's not real. It's not relevant. It's not provocative and thus, it's not thought provoking. It's imitation meat, like calling canned ham a steak (and while canned meat is all the rage in this early industrial era, I have a hunch we'll someday use it as a pejorative term for unwanted letters that clutter our mailboxes).

The biggest issue is that Ed Helper doesn't know my students as well as I do. Ultimately, that's the real issue. Teaching is a relational gig and as long as people outsource it to guys like Ed or to a program like Pencil Island, the students will suffer.

*   *   *

"How is your battle going against Pencil Island?" Mr. Brown asks as we park our horses and prepare for the day ahead of us.

"I'm recognizing that it's not simply an issue of the tools. The tools are neutral. It's about the learning. It's about matching the right tools with the best practices. Then, and only then, will we have progress," I explain.

Mr. Brown reminds me that it's a common belief that the right technology can fix some part of humanity that is broken. "It's the lie of Babel. It's the myth of Icarus. It's the notion that if we build it high enough, we can fix something inherently broken in this world."

Ruth sees it less in terms of a drug and more in terms of a byproduct of industrialization. She says that some day teachers will be turned into machinery, making "data-driven" decisions (rather than "data informed") and that the enemy will be anyone who tries to fight for student and teacher autonomy. She says that the whole system is built like a factory from worksheet packets to school bells to students in tidy little lines marching mindlessly to class. She thinks that even the most progressive media will fall in love with quick-fix reformers who will pose with broomstick props before a national magazine.

"There's a lot of money to be made on a child's mind. It's the best place to colonize, because it's a resource that they can extract for a lifetime," she laments.

*   *   *

My principal pulls me aside one afternoon. "Techno-Tommy, we need to talk." I appreciate the subtle warning. Any time the word "need" is used, it means I'm in trouble.

"Tom, I don't like the way you talked to the consultant from Pencil Island," he says squinting through his very dated monocle.

"The man's a snake oil salesman, not a consultant." I explain.

"Look, I know you don't trust businessmen, but this isn't time to pull a Coxey's Army stunt. Not all business is bad. I don't mind if you're a Populist, but education is a business and we need to recognize it as such," he explains.

"It's not a business and I'm not an executive. This is called public education for a reason. I serve, because I care about my students. I am a civil servant representing my community and I don't think my community wants to sell a child's mind to a wolf in professional clothing," I tell him.

He turns away for a moment and then says, very deliberately, "All curriculum costs money."

"That's not the issue. Yes, books cost money. But this man has a whole system set up designed to teach rote skills and make him a fortune. He's selling bad ideas."

"Pencil Island is amazing, Tom. Information is broken down into consumable parts for children," my principal explains.

"Consumable. That's the problem. Children should be thinking, not consuming," I respond.

"This is the Age of Industry. We need to prepare future

factory workers. We need compliant workers. We're pulling out of an economic panic and we have to educate our way into becoming an industrial nation."

"If that's the case, why bother with school? I hear most factories will hire kids as young as five or six. We won't even need to turn the school into a factory. I think Rockefeller could hook them up with a low-skilled job. Might as well start them early when their hands are nimble," I say sarcastically.

"Do you suggest that we give them an archaic education? Set them up to be liberal arts majors. How many jobs these days are asking for experts in philosophy?" he asks.

"No, I'm suggesting that we give them a Twentieth Century Education that helps them become part of the Creative Class. Let them be innovators and thinkers rather than factory workers. Setting kids down in isolation to fill out worksheet packets seems like a step in the wrong direction."

The school decides to buy Pencil Island for the slower readers and I end up apologizing, not for what I said, but for how I said it.

*   *   *

Paul warned me about this back when I began this journey. He said that I would grow bitter and angry about how money is spent on pencil-based learning.

"When you find yourself getting angry like that, remember that change is not something you enforce. It's something that grows. So grow your own garden. Go underground if necessary, but focus on using the tools you have rather than dreaming up something you don't have."

CHAPTER THREE

So, I start to focus on my own classroom.

When my students write to congressional representatives about a pressing issue in our society, I am amazed by the art of persuasion rather than griping about the Edison Projector that wastes our valuable school resources. When I watch students scribble out notes for their debates, I find myself amazed, not by the quality of paper, but by the power of persuasion.

I start noticing myself shifting from asking, "Are they using the paper correctly?" to "What are my students learning? How do they feel about this? Is this relevant to how they live?"

As I make this shift, I have the students work toward re-purposing an empty field as a community garden. They use charts to figure out the finances, write letters to get donations, organize the information in their own binders and create amazing sketches using some pretty complex geometric thinking.

A few times, they actually pick up the slates and design parts of their project using a traditional method. Because the novelty of one-to-one pencils is wearing off, they are open to using more traditional methods without it feeling like a punishment.

After taking a few weekends to plant the garden, a student says to me, "I really liked this unit. And you know, it had nothing to do with the pencils."

Another student adds, "I agree. It's the first time I was able to create something that connects to the community."

Still, the district office classroom visitors fail to see any of this. Instead, they take notes on whether I use my SmartChart or how many students have pencils and whether or not they keep the pencils well sharpened. I want to scream, "It's not the chart that makes them smart! It's not the pencils, even! Yes, I love the pencils, but it's their minds. Stop for a minute and observe. Really observe. Set your papers down and listen to the conversation. It's beautiful, folks. And you can't see it, because you suffer from the same technophilia tunnel vision that I slip into when I'm not careful."

*   *   *

I am standing in front of my SmartChart, flipping through the slides. The students are nodding their heads and I'm offering a passionate lecture on Jacksonian Democracy and whether his human rights violations toward Native Americans nullifies Jackson's hero status.

Mr. Brown stands in the back and observes. It's his prep period and he's hiding from Gertrude the CANDY LAND Specialist. When I pass out the paper and pencils, students begin scribbling their thoughts.

"What did you think?" I ask.

"I saw a lot of heads nod," he tells me.

"Yeah, they seemed really into it," I respond.

"They were falling asleep, Tom."

"I knew it. I practically wrote a novel on some of the chart paper. I should have gone with the three by three rule and the slides could have had more . . . " I say.

"No, that wasn't the problem. Your problem wasn't your paper but your pedagogy. You stood and lectured. You failed to interact. I've seen you lead discussions. Slides could have enhanced the discussion, but you allowed a projector and some ginormous paper replace you as the teacher," he explains.

It's in this moment that realize that if I'm not careful, I become just like the vendors. I lose touch just as bad as the well-intentioned Ed, who is, at this stage, doing his very best to help students, despite their refusal to do his worksheets. I'm a con artist creating a pencil island where I'm the dictator.

*   *   *

It's the last day of the quarter and things are beginning to take root in the garden. I hold the earth in my hands and let it slip through my fingers. I love what we accomplish with our pencils, but I have this vague sense that we are losing something as we move forward.

Let them look.

Let them peer into the garden.

Consider the lilies, right?

It's not exactly a twentieth century skill, but I'd like my students to stop and consider and maybe even find a level of contentment in the process.

"It's impressive what you've accomplished," a parent says.

"But we didn't. Not really. Call it grace. I know that has a religious connotation, but I have no better word for it," I say.

The lie of the Industrial Age is that we plan it. The machinery suggests we have total control over it. We simply set up the structures, plug in the right medium and create a progressive model.

The garden tells me otherwise. We planned, yes. We planted a

PENCIL ME IN

seed. But the growth wasn't ours. The change was organic. All of a sudden those agrarian metaphors of education don't seem so trite. Not when you hold a fresh tomato in your hands.

We have more squash than I imagined we would. The lettuce is starting to grow, too. The herb garden explodes with scent after a late October storm. I inhale the clean, crisp air.

Grace.

We didn't earn any of it.

CHAPTER FOUR

From Toys to Tools

I'm in a "behavior meeting," with a parent, a child and three other teachers. Under the guise of "finding solutions," each teacher blames and shames until the boy cries. (Occasionally teachers will actually delight in this, believing that shame leads to a change in direction, when, in fact, it leads to perfectionism, rebellion and ultimately hedging your bets and wearing masks so that no one ever knows you)

"He's doing well for me. I teach all the subjects except for the electives," I explain.

"He only does well because of the pencils," another teacher says.

"I really think it's because he and I have found a way to get along," I add.

PENCIL ME IN

Another teacher says, "I wish I had a set of pencils. Maybe he would behave for me. I know he loves pencils. I guess we can't all have it our way."

"I see your point. However, I'm not sure the pencils are the thing that makes it mea. . ."

"Don't get defensive, Tom. He loves your class for the pencils. That's a good thing. At least he doesn't interrupt you with stupid questions. In gym class . . ."

His voice trails off and I check out. Turns out this meeting was meant to shame and blame the student rather than develop solutions that will allow him to thrive. What he doesn't realize is that pencils will be exciting for a day. Any new technology is like that. We have a phonograph that the students fell in love with for a week. We have access to a telegraph that we use on occasion.

Ultimately, though, it is about trust and purpose. This child trusts me, because I don't shame him. In fact, the one time I yelled at him, I apologized and he responded with humility and strength. He trusts me, because I know him and I know him, because I take the time to listen. This child sees meaning and purpose in what we do in class. I try not to waste his time with meaningless work and in return he doesn't waste my time with meaningless chatter.

None of that requires a pencil.

When the meeting ends, the teachers walk out first. The child is sitting with his face buried in his hands, tears streaming down. An angry mother sits beside him.

As he gets up to leave, he says, "I don't just like your class for the pencils. I like pencils. But I like your class because it's fun.

No, sometimes it's really boring and, I don't know. I don't know why I like your class, but it isn't just the pencils."

"I know," I tell him.

*   *   *

At the start of the year, I viewed pencils as a magical talisman that would transform every student into a self-motivated learner. I believed that the Pencil Natives would grab hold of a pencil and start creating amazing works of poetry and stories that would change the world. I thought that the simple existence of paper would mean clarity of thought, critical thinking and logic in persuasive writing.

It worked for a day or two, but eventually the pencil novelty wore off and students realized that they were working with tools. Many of my students had used pencils at home. However, many had spent their hours playing Hang Man or sending texts through the pen pal network and now I was asking them to solve equations and write full paragraphs. It was a hard paradigm shift for them to make.

Looking back, I recognize that I was no different than the students. I confused novelty and fun with meaning and depth.

*   *   *

We begin a unit with the students completing a Venn diagram. A few students write comments on the margins of one another's notebooks, but they are generally on-task. However, I notice one of my top students using her finger to smudge pencil lines.

"Gladys, I need to see you." I warn her about the learning tool concept and moments later she sits alone smudging pencil again.

PENCIL ME IN

"Grab a slate. You'll be using that today," I tell her.

She finishes the assignment with a slate. As they line up for lunch, she asks me, "What's the point in pencils if we can't even have fun with them?"

I ignore her. It's the best I can do to avoid screaming. Nobody told me about this side of pencil integration.

In the staff lounge, I share this incident with Mr. Brown. "Was my lesson just not engaging enough? Did I fail to motivate her?"

Mr. Brown surprises me with his response, "Dude, chill. This stuff happens with slates, does it not? We like to believe that kids will always do what they are supposed to do. But the reality is that they are just like us. They want to play and they want to learn and sometimes they are addicted to fun and we have to redirect them."

"Should I have created a lesson that was more fun?"

"I don't think so. However, when this happens with slates, I don't take the slates away. You just don't take away tools. It's our job to teach content not obedience," he adds.

At this point our Vocational Learning teacher stepped in. "Tom, tools require responsibility. Sure, motivation is part of it. But the goal is for students to learn. If your lesson was meaningful and most students were engaged, that wasn't the problem. Some kids are immature . . . Okay, all kids are immature, just at different times. When they can come back to the situation and be mature, we allow them to use the tools."

"So, is it right to punish a kid for that?"

"It's not punishment, it's a preventative measure to keep things from escalating. If a kid is messing around with a saw, I take it away from him. The important thing is that the student has another chance tomorrow."

Mr. Brown adds, "I still don't think we should teach students lessons by taking away supplies."

"What would you have done, Mr. Brown?"

"I would have given her the option of finishing the Venn diagram at another time and found away to incorporate her picture into the lesson. If she wants to be creative in how she uses a tool, why not see where she goes with it? But maybe that's a stretch."

*   *   *

"I can't believe Mrs. Jackson threw away my document because I didn't have my name on it. I worked really hard, left it on my desktop and now it's gone," a student complains.

"Did you talk to her about it?" I ask.

"She said that in the real world an employer would never accept work from an employee who forgets a name. She said that if I were to submit a time sheet with no name, I wouldn't get paid. I will thank her some day for preparing me for life. Besides, she's not a detective, she's a teacher."

"She has a point. What did you say to her?"

"I told her that I'm not an adult and I wouldn't expect her to play hopscotch well, either, since she's not a kid. I told her that I will work hard to remember next time and I'll make it a habit to save my document from the trash by writing my name on it at the beginning."

"Makes sense," I say.

PENCIL ME IN

"She told me that she'll still give me a zero and I told her she wasn't being fair. So, when she said 'Life isn't fair' I told her that it's a teacher's job to fight on the side of fairness. That's when she kicked me out and told me that someday I'll thank her for teaching me a life lesson," he explains.

I tell him to sit down in the Corner of Shame. It's part of our School-wide Discipline Program called Shame-Based Organizational Behavior Process or SOB Process.

Minutes later, Mrs. Jackson sends me a note explaining that this child is banned from using pencils for the rest of the year. She calls the learning tools "a privilege," which is odd, because I can't imagine her telling a child that he can't use a slate or that he is banned from all algorithms.

Eventually, I let this child join my class in our own pencil-integrated lesson. When Mrs. Jackson asks about my defiance of her orders, I tell her that I couldn't read her note, because it didn't have her name on it. After all, this is the real world and if this were a time card, she wouldn't get paid and besides, life is unfair and it's not my job to fight for fairness. When she protests that I should recognize her handwriting, I tell her that I'm not a detective, I'm a teacher.

As she storms off, I tell her, "You'll thank me for this someday. I'm teaching you a valuable life lesson."

Later that evening, I debrief it with Ruth.

"Sure, what's up?"

I tell her all about what happened and I add, "Perhaps I was a bit too harsh, but I'm convinced that we shouldn't take away learning tools for unrelated disciplinary reasons. Sometimes trouble-makers don't even get a chance."

"I know what you mean. A teacher will say, 'Timmy's just not mature enough for a pencil yet,' meaning 'I don't trust him and I'm scared he'll snap one in half.' If spoken with just the right calm, condescending voice, even Timmy begins to believe that he is not entitled to use a tool designed for his own education," she says.

"So you agree with me?" I ask.

"Yes and no. You brought up a great point. Teachers sometimes forget that they're kids. And they forget that it's a learning experience and not a privilege," she says.

"Exactly! That's the point. It's not a privilege. I don't want to take away a child's education for a failure to follow a procedure. Nor should we reward a student who is done with slate-work to go to another table to play with the pencils," I explain.

"I get it, Tom. As long as teachers use this approach they will perpetuate a myth that pencils are toys rather than tools and are meant for amusement rather than learning. But . . ."

"What?" I ask incredulously.

She shrugs her shoulders. "I've been in Mrs. Jackson's class before, Tom. She's a great teacher and she's a compassionate person. Punishing her for her mistake is no different than what she has done with that child. Just think about it."

*   *   *

The principal pulls me aside and says, "Tom, I'm not a counselor. I'm not a psychologist. I'm not even a phrenologist, so you won't see me trying analyze the bumps on your head to see what you were thinking. But we need to resolve some conflict."

"What's the matter?" I ask.

"I want you to know that Mrs. Jackson is in my office right now," he says.

"Be easy on her. I don't think she realized how harsh she was being toward him. I mean, kicking him out like that. Sending him to solitary confinement and all for something that an adult . . ."

"You need to talk to her. I didn't want you to feel like it was a trap when you walked in," he says.

The meeting begins rough, with Mrs. Jackson crying and pointing her finger at my face. She lectures me about being unprofessional and I tell her that being a professional means respecting kids.

"Kicking a student out for a name on a paper is also unprofessional," I explain.

"You have to understand that we can't coddle kids. They have to know that in the real world they'll need to learn to get along and respect authority and remember details. Seriously, what boss would possibly . . ."

Finally our principal speaks up. "You just said that in the real world kids will need to learn to get along and yet I'm having to hold a mediation in my office right now. As I see it, you're both right. Mr. Johnson, you have every right to suggest that a child will be forgetful and that shame simply brings out anger and rebellion. Mrs. Jackson, you're right that children need consequences and it is our job to prepare them for the reality of a world that doesn't look like a bunch of cuddly bunnies and 'great job' stickers."

It's silent again, but this time out of a shared sense of remorse. I offer an awkward, clunky apology. Mrs. Jackson holds out her arm for one of those camp-counselor-side-hugs.

Later that day, the principal pulls me aside. "Tom, one thing you don't see is her fear."

"Fear? Are you crazy?"

"Slates have been working for her. Now she has to adjust. And not only adjust but she's behind the curve. How hard is that for her? You missed it. You missed her courage. She tried something really new to her and it failed. Can't you see that?"

I nod my head.

*   *   *

Later that day, Mrs. Jackson explains, "I guess I get nervous and uncomfortable with paper and pencil. My rules change. I get uptight. That kid I timed out wasn't a bad kid by any means. In fact, I apologized to him the minute he returned to my classroom. I just feel like I'm wandering in a maze right now and everything that seemed normal five years ago is no longer enough."

"I get what you're saying," I tell her.

"Teaching was always confusing. But the confusion was a labyrinth with multiple options and a slow pace. Now it's this maze with all these sharp cut-off points and dead-ends. I'm more confused than ever."

Mrs. Jackson is a phenomenal teacher and yet her veteran status often works against her. People see the pencils and papers in my class and call me "innovative" and "forward thinking," and they pull her aside for condescending discussions about the need to move into the twentieth century. The reason she was acting out of character had less to do with student behavior and more to do with how she handled shame.

Here's the rub: Pencils geeks need her. True, she gets a little nervous around a pencil sharpener. Perhaps she grows uptight when kids forget names on papers. However, she is not easily wooed by a shiny gadgetry. Instead, learning impresses her and hence she has a contagious love of literature that her children seem to catch.

What if we changed pencil-integrated professional development so that she became one of the experts? What if, instead of sending her to a pencil workshop, we used job-embedded training that allowed her to use her expertise on pedagogy coupled with another teacher's expertise in the new tools? What if we redefined "innovation" to be less about tools and more about quality craftsmanship?

*   *   *

Mr. Brown walks into my room in a fury. "Can you believe we have to take time out of social studies to teach Career Readiness Achievement Program?"

"I'm sure the districts spent barrels of money on it, what with all the worksheets and workbooks and . . ."

"You nailed it. They're worksheets and workbooks, but nothing is a thinkbook or thinksheet anymore. It's about productivity and results and not the cognitive process anymore. Might as well turn them into machines," I say.

"I'm upset with the conflict of interest. Am I really supposed to believe that a program developed by Carnegie can be trusted? Can I really separate out Carnegie the corrupt robber baron from Carnegie the educational reformer? Yes, it's fine that he wants to give back, but it feels a bit like robbing a house and then returning a few pairs of slacks and some silverware," he explains.

He pulls out a pencil and adds, "It has nothing to do with pencils. You know that I've been doing two to three pencil-based lessons a week. I'm getting used to it."

"What scares me is that teachers seem to love this program simply because it uses technology. So, for a day they'll have access to a camera and through the entire unit, they'll have paper and pencil. They're using novelty to sell us CRAP."

Paul the Preindustrial Poet thinks the best way to prepare someone for the workforce is to prepare someone for life. He says that most factory skills can be learned in the first two or three weeks, but life skills take a lifetime to learn. Paul thinks that some day in the near future we won't be making gas lamps or buggy whips and kids who learned those skills will be lost as we shift into a newer, electric-based economy.

"But teach them to think and they'll learn any new skill," he adds.

I'm thinking he and Mr. Brown both have a point here. We're educating eighth graders. Do they really need job preparation right now? Is this really the time to have them develop a Career Readiness Plan?

"So, Mr. Brown, what is your plan? Are you just going to play ignorant and claim you never had training on it?"

"No, I have another idea. They'll fill out the worksheets alright. You'll see," he smirks.

For the most part, I abandon the worksheets. We breeze through them quickly and then I break students up into small groups to discuss the question, "What are the elements of a good career?" After the brainstorm, I present career philosophies:

- Vocational: based upon one's identity, beliefs and values. It's the notion that who you are guides what you do (a sense of calling to it)
- Hedonist: find a job that is enjoyable, fun or pleasurable.
- Economic: a job is based upon money. The higher the pay, the better the job.
- Recognition: the best job is one where a person will receive honor, recognition, fame or accolades.
- Humanitarian: here the idea is to make a difference in the lives of others

Students engage in a debate about the merits of each philosophy and the question of whether someone can truly pursue multiple career philosophies and find contentment. Afterward, a student pulls me aside as the small groups work on their pros and cons chart.

"If there are all these reasons for having a career and our school wants to get us job-ready in the future, why are we only following the economic philosophy? Why don't we make a difference as a school? Why don't we talk about identity and values and beliefs?"

CHAPTER FOUR

"Some people don't think that's important. They see it as fluff. Shouldn't we pursue the core knowledge?"

He responds, "It seems like answering the question of why we work a job in the first place would be at the core of all of our knowledge."

As the students work on a plog post describing their career philosophy preferences, I hear shouting from Mr. Brown's classroom.

"Faster, I say! It's not about quality! It's numbers! It's data! We need to win this race! It's a race to the top, I tell you! A race to the top! Only one worker will earn the ultimate reward! It will mean innovation! And our company will not have any losers being left behind!"

"But Mr. Brown, the work is looking sloppy and everything we do looks identical!" a child complains.

"Welcome to the edu-factory," he responds. "It's a model forged by factory reform. We're running a faster society where some day a family of five will have to earn two incomes to fill their homes up with cheap plastic crap made by kids like you," he says.

Students are in an assembly line filling out one line on each of their worksheets. On the sideline are students who want a piece of the grade as well. "You sir, do you want to work in this edu-factory? I'll pay you a C for the work. Right now you're failing. Take a C!"

The child simply nods.

"Excellent! We have to make sure that no child is left behind!"

PENCIL ME IN

The students sigh.

"Alright, everybody, your grade is now a C! We only have so many points to spread around. But we can now hire two new workers. And our investors will earn a higher yield. Just wait for awhile and the points might trickle down to you."

A child volunteers to work for a D and Mr. Brown fires another worker who refuses a C. Finally, two more workers begin to whisper to one another. "We quit. We'll fail this unit if we need to."

This leads to a chain reaction as the students begin to go on strike. As my students discuss career philosophies, his students talk about unions and free markets, wages and fairness and eventually meander into why one would work a job at all.

Neither of us taught the same lesson. I might steal his idea next year and I know he plans to use my career philosophies tomorrow. We share. That's the idea of common knowledge and common standards. It's horizontal. Our paper and pencil integration is natural and fluid and based upon our own expertise. We're two craftsmen wielding their tools creatively.

Give us a program and we'll be programmed. The results will be uniform, but we'll miss the chance to be innovative. Give us the freedom to share what has worked and we'll grow together, each of us learning new ways to using various tools.

So, it's the third day of our unit and I take Mr. Brown's idea of a factory game. I spend some time developing a program for learning about economics. It's a market simulation game, where students graph their own investments and interact with one another. Throughout this process, they write reflections, send messages and join a pen pal network.

Gertrude steps into my room and asks, "Why are they playing a game instead of learning?"

"It's not a game. It's a research-based, student-centered, interactive learning activity constructed to integrate pencils into a core knowledge environment." If only Gertrude had only brought her Buzzword Bingo card!

A student walks up to us, "Mr. Johnson, I love this game. Why can't we play games more often? This is fun!"

Gertrude gives me the death stare.

I explain to her that the students use math, reading and writing. I hand her a short example of this and say, "They are actually spending more time using their core curriculum skills than they would be if I stood here and lectured them on economic theory. Listen, my goal was not fun. A pencil isn't a toy. It's a tool. We're just using it in a way that's more interactive."

"You can't be playing games," she reminds me. "School has always been about work, not play. The bottom line isn't fun."

She paces around the room and asking economic questions to students. "They seem to know what they are learning," she says with a slight smile that almost makes me wonder if she is human after all. Later, though, I hear her complain about me in the staff lounge. She calls me arrogant and obsessed with trying to make the kids like me. What she misses, though, is the power of games.

For millennia, it was a cultural universal that games existed for learning. True, children had fun, but the games were designed to teach both social and physical skills. Children learned to be warriors, how to govern, how to access cultural narratives all through the act of play. In fact, Plato theorized that one could learn more about a person through an hour of play than a lifetime of conversation.

Even in America, where we have shifted toward a sit-in-your-desk-and-shut-up-and-learn model, our games become methods of accessing these cultural skill sets. One the darker side, Simon Says teaches social conformity and prepares small kids for the prison-like environment of their future careers. Dodge Ball teaches Social Darwinism and Crony Capitalism. Hide and Go Seek teaches children that transparency is overrated. Best run and hide from others. After all, this is the building block of many grown-up relationships.

On the flip side, our games teach the best of American values. Hide and Go Seek helps teach autonomy and creativity. Simon Says teaches listening skills and proves to kids that language can be powerful. Dodge Ball helps with teamwork and allows kids to see the value of throwing things at people for sheer enjoyment.

*   *   *

When the game ends, students debrief the information in their plogs. After words, we set our pencils down and talk. On some level, it feels like waking up for a daze. Students debate the pros and cons of a market system, talk about the risks of speculation and relate this to the economic crash of last year.

CHAPTER FOUR

The pencil smudge girl from yesterday raises her hand, "I think there is a danger in playing this game, but I'm glad we played it."

"Can you elaborate on that?" I ask.

"I think the people in Wall Street got suckered into the same vortex that we were just in. They got selfish and that led to the Panic a few years back. It became a game to win. I think that's how it is for some of the people who run Wall Street."

All of this has me reconsidering the notion of fun. I don't want my students to be amusement-addicts who play a violent Hang Man game or throw wads of paper out of boredom. I want students to use pencils as a tool. However, I'm realizing that games can be a tool for learning. I'm left feeling conflicted and confused. Perhaps technology can be a toy and the game can spur deeper reflection.

* * *

I'm sitting at home with my daughter. She's tossing a ball at the fence. The ball has been the dragon that attacked her fortress made of blocks. Now it's a magic ball that will lose its fairy dust if it falls on the ground more than once. She's playing and learning and there isn't much of a divide at this age.

Perhaps there shouldn't ever be such a rigid divide. Perhaps when my students ask, "Can we play games?" or "Can't we have fun?" the answer doesn't have to be "these are tools not toys." Maybe the answer can be, "Maybe they are tools, but maybe they're also toys. Sometimes it will be fun. Sometimes it will be difficult. But I will always try and make sure it's meaningful."

PENCIL ME IN

And it has me thinking that maybe innovation happens, not because we use our tools appropriately but because we play with them. We hack them. We change them. We use them in ways they weren't intended to be used and in the process, they become better tools.

CHAPTER FIVE
Who Owns Your Voice?

We meet in the district office conference room. Within minutes, I'm already having a difficult time keeping the classroom perspective. I am surrounded by sketches of inspiring people climbing mountains, with words like "courage" and "endurance." I can see how a person would lose courage in the large bulwark of bureaucracy, but I'm not sure the poster will be of much help. Endurance, however, shouldn't be a problem. Not when they provide you with a bottomless cup of coffee.

At one point, we get into the question of paper usage. "I need to know what type of paper we should use," the edu-crat explains.

"I think we can go with lined paper for us and let kids decide if they need any other type," I chime in.

PENCIL ME IN

A teacher voices her concerns, "That's not going to happen while I'm here. There are way too many platforms. How am I supposed to grade papers written on so many different types of paper?"

I respond, "What if it's not about format but about learning? So, a kid wants to use the free lined paper donated by the folks who design paper. What's that term? Freeware? Maybe another kid wants to use the fancy iParchment that the professional artists use. Perhaps another one wants the MicroPaper that they use in the corporate world. One kid wants wide ruled and another uses college ruled. Is that such a bad thing?"

The district representative offers his perspective, "I think the mere availability of multiple paper platforms makes it confusing when you ask for paper help from the district. Can you really expect our technicians to know how to handle ripped iParchment one day and then your Linus paper the next day. They'll quit."

A teacher adds, "Or, how about this: What if a student is using illegally-secured paper that he stole from a paper supplier? These are very real concerns."

"I'll encourage students to use the free paper that is available to the public within the paper commons. It's a great place where you can take paper when you need. And as far as paper help, shouldn't a paper expert understand all paper platforms?"

The teacher glares at me and says, "If you think I'm going to accept work created with different types of paper, you're insane. What if a student gets it from a spiral notebook and I get frizzies on my desk? I can't have frizzies."

CHAPTER FIVE

"So, you tell that student to cut and paste the work from the first paper into your paper platform. It's not that hard to do, really."

The edu-crat turns to me and explains, "Tom, I think you're outnumbered on this one. Our district only uses iParchment. I know it's expensive, but it's top-quality and it will last longer. Besides, it's what the professionals use. If students want to bring in their own paper, it has to be iParchment."

"You say you want creative and imaginative teachers. You want us to think outside the box and then you get angry when we don't have students follow your rigid platform. It's the same thing with the pencil-based curriculum. We're stuck using packets of worksheets," I argue.

"There's flexibility in it. Read the Teacher Workbook. Each lesson has at least three Extension Activities you can consider. If you want anarchy, go back to a Haymarket Square Riot," he says, touching a nerve. It wasn't anarchy. It was more than that. We wanted a voice.

I still want a voice.

As I leave, I fail to say what is going through my mind: What if we stopped investing in curriculum and started investing in our children's minds? What if we quit treating the students as a resource that we own?

*   *   *

The school pencil teacher pulls me aside in the staff lounge, "Mr. Johnson, I'm concerned with your eighth graders. Did you teach them how to write properly?"

PENCIL ME IN

"Yes sir, I did. Are they having a hard time?" I ask.

"Well, I'm concerned that some of them have been using shorthand and abbreviations," he explains.

"That doesn't surprise me. They often hand one another messages written in shorthand before and after school. Apparently they even set the messages on the walls of their friend's homes," Mr. Brown mentions.

"You mean they leave comments for everyone to read right there on a wall?" the pencil teacher asks.

"Yes. Personally, I blame it on those Pen Pal networks they've joined," Gertrude adds.

I stay diplomatic and say, "I'll work harder on teaching them proper grammar and punctuation."

Upon further reflection, I have a few thoughts. Shorthand is simply another register. People can switch between casual slang, casual, formal English and academic registers without one register "bleeding over" into the other. A true writer can write a persuasive paper and a poem without losing the ability to do either. Shorthand is designed to be efficient and has its place. Some day, secretaries will use it throughout the corporate world.

Language is fluid. It changes constantly, which is why I can't think of the last time I voted for a member of "Congrefs." Shorthand can have its place in the classroom, which is why teachers shouldn't ban it, but instead teach students about the time and place to use it.

I leave the conversation feeling confused. Who owns a child's voice? And why, if our goal is to empower students toward democratic thinking, do we focus on a model of censoring? It has me questioning grades and the random check marks I place. It has me thinking about our garden, about growth, about the need to observe rather than judge.

If I believe in pencils, then I have to believe there is a chance to change. That is essentially the message of that medium. It's the idea change is a necessary part of life. If I believe that work is worth keeping and modifying, I have to believe the goal is individual mastery.

I start thinking of the ways that I censor student voices. I mark up their documents with redlined comments and then place an arbitrary number at the top, based mostly upon whether or not I enjoy what they wrote.

So, I start a new pencil project with them. It's a class magazine (think "shared journal" rather than the profiteering yellow journalism of Hearst).

I ask them first to leave comments on a plog answering the question, "How do you feel when you have a writing assignment in school?"

I cringe at the words "scared" and "nervous" and "dread."

"What if you chose the format and the topic? What if there were no deadlines? You could simply publish it when you feel that it is worth reading."

We agree to start a class plog. The students aptly name the plog *The Voice Collective*.

"Should we make our class plog public?"

.

PENCIL ME IN

"Wouldn't that be dangerous? I mean, wouldn't you worry about creepy people?"

"Maybe," another student interjects, "but I wonder if that's mostly hype. I mean, we let kids sing solos and do concerts for the public, right? And our school already has a baseball team. What's the difference?"

Another student adds, "Actually, a plog seems a little more anonymous. At a baseball game, they see you in person, learn your entire name and have physical access to you. A plog just means they have access to your public thoughts."

"Anyone in the world could visit this site," I point out.

"Do you really think anyone in the world is just going to randomly find our plogs?" a student asks. "No, they have to be searching for it. And if someone across the globe wants to take a boat to our great city and read the work of a bunch of eighth-graders, I say go for it!"

"What if you accidentally said something personal?" another student asks.

"Am I going to quit going to a diner because someone might eavesdrop?" another student asks.

Another student points out, "I'd like to know what people think of my writing. If someone leaves a bad comment on the margins, I can always erase it. That's the beauty of a pencil."

Finally, Anne, a typically shy child, raises her hand and says, "I don't want my posts to be public. I think they belong to the classroom. They should be read by us. These walls aren't all bad. They define our community. I wrote with my classmates in mind.

If I knew the public wanted to read my plog, I would have written it a little differently."

I quickly develop a compromise, "What if we took this route? What if we played it safe at first and created a three-tiered approach? We could have *The Voice Collective* as a class. We could then share our personal plog with the class and then have a separate private journal."

The class agrees with this solution, but then a boy pulls me aside and says, "Mr. Johnson, I think we should get to choose if we make our personal plog private or public. I think every student should have ownership of his or her voice."

Another student pulls me aside and reminds me, "Students get in trouble for talking too much. Why aren't schools dealing with the kids who are too scared to speak up?"

*   *   *

On an early autumn morning a student greets me with a horrible story, "Mr. Johnson, someone wrote something really mean on our plog."

I look at the margins and read the long, convoluted, well-educated rhetoric against immigrants combined with a more colloquial string of insults, "Cheaters, border hopers, criminals." For what it's worth, I don't think they were referring to "hope" in writing "hopers," but I could be wrong.

"We're Irish, yes, but American too. We're not illegals. Not any more illegal than anyone else who came here to take land from the Indians. We just came here to work," she tells me.

PENCIL ME IN

I pull out my pencil and erase the marks; forever wiping out the anonymous comment from the public memory of the event. I am the Editor, the Censor who must decipher between mean-spirited attacks and passionate criticism. Or perhaps I am the protector who will not let some anonymous critic silence my students' voices.

I ask the students if we should allow anonymous comments.

"People hide when they are anonymous. They attack, because it is a surprise attack. It's secret," a girl says.

"It's like the KKK. They cover themselves in a white sheet, spout out hate and they don't have to be transparent." A bit of an extreme metaphor, I admit, but I could see his point.

"I think we should allow people to be anonymous. At least it's honest when they do that. So, people hate the Irish. At least this way we know it. No one is pretending."

The debate continues until a student says, "I think we're on the wrong track altogether. I think it's hypocritical for us to require people to state their first and last name and yet we post our work with just our first names."

"We do that to protect you. Remember, employers can go back and search public records. It's all part of your public footprint."

The student responds, "I know that, Mr. Johnson. But shouldn't that be exactly what we want people to see? Okay, so imagine someone takes a photograph of me drinking at a party or entering a burlesque theater and I get hired by a member of the Temperance Movement. That can be real damaging if they find that on the pen pal networks. So, why not let them see the good side of me instead? Why not let them see that since the eighth grade I have been doing community service and I have cared about conservation?"

It has me thinking about anonymity. Perhaps no one should be anonymous in pencil postings. Perhaps the veil we wear in plogs and pen pal networks can work both ways - hiding the good and allowing us to commit acts of cruelty without facing consequences.

I want my students to own their voice. I want them to use whatever tool is necessary to refine it – whether the tool is a spelling checker or a shorthand message or a pen pal network or plog. I want my students to speak boldly without fear of angry comments.

I want my students to recognize that while the system is rigged by huge paper and pencil companies, their voice cannot be bought. Yes, I want them to know how to use a pencil. But I would rather them learn how to use their voice – whether it is aloud, on a slate or with a pencil.

I also have lingering fears. Plogs are permanent. One's voice remains forever. What if that contributes to the death of childhood? What if the constant interaction with the adult world and the sense of responsibility we demand of them as they use their pencils goes against the notion of childhood and the concept of making mistakes on the road toward adulthood?

CHAPTER SIX
Quit Stealing Our Tools

It's a chilly October afternoon, the time of year when everything seems to be dying and the earth itself feels in an early rapid decay. We're edgy, feeling intuitively the dying light and understanding that it will be another half year before a celebratory rebirth. It's fitting, then, that this is the time of the year when we receive our bad news.

Mr. Brown pulls me aside to discuss our field trip plans. "They canceled both of our field trips, Tom. Can you believe it? We planned out our lessons to fit those particular locations and out of nowhere, they just blocked the sites."

"They can't do that. We had parent permission slips. We spent our time developing whole projects around it," I explain.

CHAPTER SIX

"Yeah, apparently a kid in another school wandered off to another site. I guess they were on Main Street and he ditched to watch a baseball game. He started talking to kids at another school. Eventually, he ran off and saw an adult show," Mr. Brown says.

"So, what does that mean for us?" I ask.

"We can't go anywhere, pretty much. You know how we wanted to go to a motion picture, right?" he asks.

"Yeah, there's a short film about the Arctic," I say.

"Well, they're worried that kids might wander off and try and see a peep show instead," Mr. Brown says.

"Isn't that an issue of classroom management?" I ask.

"You would think. One might assume that the teacher who failed would go to some training," he says

"Or maybe the kids would be reprimanded," I say.

He nods his head, "It gets worse, though. You know how we were going to take them to see the orchestra, right?"

"They're canceling that?" I ask.

"Turns out the orchestra is next to a place that plays rag time and rag time is dangerous stuff," he shakes his head.

"Seriously? There's more sex and violence in Shakespeare and yet kids are forced to read his plays," I explain.

"I know," he says.

"Okay, okay. So, what about the museum. We get to go there, right?"

"Nope. It turns out that as the kids wander around and search the images they can stumble upon some of that dangerous Renaissance art that has nudity," he says.

"Can't a teacher filter out the experience so that they go to the correct images? And can't we teach kids to understand respectful and tasteful nude art?" I ask.

"Well, the corridors are still open and so the district is worried about it. These are Victorian times, my friend. Everything has to be hyper-clean. In fact, they're talking about canceling all field trips for fear that a kid would run into a predator in public."

"Wow, Victorian times indeed!"

My wife reminds me that it was only a few months back when I took the paper and pencil away from a student for behavioral reasons.

"What motivated you back then?" she asks.

"Fear. I was scared that I would lose control of the class. I was scared it would degenerate into a class full of Hang Man," I admit.

"Fear and control. Is it possible that you're not entirely different from the district?" she asks.

*   *   *

Our plog-hosting site (also known as a "library") is across the street. The public can peruse the plogs, but also subscribe to them and have it sent directly to their home. Some plogs require registration to view or comment and others simply require a word verification code (It's a great device that may

CHAPTER SIX

some day ward off robots. For now, though, it works great at keeping Phil the Town Drunk from writing obscene comments when no one is looking.)

As we cross the road, we face a barricade sponsored by SiteSense. A security guard kindly tells us that the district has restricted us from this site. I stare at his baton and assume he means business. On the way back, a student tells me that it's what she expected. "Our district slogan is 'Learning for Life,' but life is the very thing they won't let us see."

"One of our values is community, yet we have huge walls that keep us in and the community out," another points out.

After school, I stop by the district office. The Assistant Superintendent of Paper-related Learning explains the issue to me.

"Oh yeah, you're supposed to publish all student work to the iSites. We paid good money and we're going to use it."

"Yes, but the Plogger site is free and easier to customize."

"But the iSites work with the iParchment and it flows seamlessly in a system. We know the company and we trust them. Besides, I heard that there might be pornographic plogs across the street. Gertrude was tell me a story about . . ."

"Look, I highly doubt it. But if there is, you can always fill out a Report Abuse card for the curator and she will throw the plog in the trash."

"It's a matter of safety, Tom," he explains.

"What do you mean?" I ask.

PENCIL ME IN

"We have a distinct code explaining how paper and pencil must be used," he adds.

"It seems like a double standard. Do they have an Acceptable Use Policy in the wood shop? I mean, it seems that they are much more likely to lose a hand in woodshop than, say, gouge out an eye using pencils."

"Shop class doesn't have the same rules. It's confined to one space," he explains.

"Do we block the choir from singing at the town square? I mean, I heard there is drinking and gambling that goes on over there."

"But that is supervised, Mr. Johnson. Your students could be meandering through a site that SiteSense considers potentially dangerous. They have a scientific process . . ."

"Science is about reason and skepticism. It's about inquiry and exploration. This is hysteria. It's not science."

"No, this is about compliance," he says. "If teachers did what they were supposed to do, this wouldn't be an issue. We have rules, because teachers abuse freedom."

I am struck by the notion that our community is afraid of all the wrong aspects of pencil and paper. No one questions the proper age and development of a child using a pencil. No one asks whether it is a good thing for a child to have a community audience at an age where they are making mistakes and learning how to function socially. No one looks at the death of an oral culture when we embrace all things print-related.

CHAPTER SIX

Instead, the district bans the tools that teachers might use to integrate pencils into the curriculum and prevents us from visiting sites we need to visit to improve learning. I'm not opposed to having some guidelines or even some paperwork. What scares me is that we get so hung up in creating structures of security that no one seems interested in protecting paper freedom. Moreover, we aren't developing enough opportunities for students to learn safety, since every safety precaution is taken ahead of time.

*   *   *

In the midst of our second quarter unit on freedom and democracy, the principal pulls me aside. "Tom, I need to talk to you about a bullying situation."

"Is it about Eunice and Gladys. I think we have that taken care of," I answer.

"It's the aftermath. Apparently some of the bullying was pencil-based," he explains.

"Yeah, I know about that," I respond.

"Well, we need to ban the pen pal networks. We can't have bullying occurring on our campus," he says.

"But some of the bullying happened in the cafeteria and we're not banning kids from eating in the cafeteria. Just yesterday I saw bullying in the library. Better ban books as well."

"But this is permanent. This leaves a record. Verbal and written bullying are different," he says.

PENCIL ME IN

"True, so doesn't that mean we have some evidence of the bullying when it occurs?"

"Yes, but it also means it lasts," he explains.

"Aren't the real lasting effects of verbal bullying just as permanent?" I ask.

"Parents are worried, Tom. There was a new report in the papers that children are using pencils for social reasons. They're sending shorthand messages, doing pen pal letters and whatnot. It's scary to many of the parents."

"Really? Students are using pencils for social interaction? So at an age when they are naturally social, when they are exploring conflict and relationships, they use the media that are available to act their age? Sounds incredibly dangerous to me," I say sarcastically.

"Look, we're banning the pen pal networks," he adds.

"I've been using them for class debates. It turns out they are a great collaborative tool," I respond.

"Well, you'll just have to find a better way for them to learn about democracy. Have them write in documents and publish them in their plogs."

"You mean the ones that are blocked by SiteSense?" I ask.

"What do you mean?" he asks.

"Yeah, the SiteSense guards showed up yesterday and cleared my cabinets of every journal. Kids can't access their own plogs," I say. "Tell me what that's all about."

"Tom, my number one priority is student safety," he responds.

Mrs. Jackson butts into the conversation while walking past the open door, "I'm not an administrator, but if I was, my number one priority would be learning rather than safety. True learning requires a balance of safety and freedom."

"So apparently if it's verbal, blame the student. If it's written, blame the pencils," I add.

Mrs. Jackson looks at both of us and adds, "Remember when I lost it that one day?"

"Yeah, but you've been moving toward integrating pencils," I add.

"I know, but that incident makes me a little more sympathetic to the scared parents. For all the talk of a twentieth century classroom, I find the biggest barrier to change is fear. You want your kids to be safe and the Unknown is always scary."

"Still, we need to be leaders rather than liability managers. In addition to asking, 'What will we risk if we do this?' we should also ask, 'What do we risk if we don't do this?'"

"It's not going to happen as long as public relations is more powerful than a learning tool," she adds.

"I'll see what I can do," the principal adds.

I decide at this point to address the school board:

Dear School Board Members:

I appreciate your desire to keep our students safe from bullying, disruptions and "anything that gets in the way of learning." However, I am concerned that your efforts have not gone far enough. You banned the Pen Pal networks and now mobile pencil devices. I get it, those tablets were very disruptive, what with kids sending shorthand messages and all.

At first, I had a negative reaction. After all, as a teacher, I would deal with the behavior rather than banning the medium. If a student is disruptive, I have a conversation with the individual rather than punishing the whole class. I've even been known to get introspective and ask myself why the student was disengaged. Can I incorporate something different in the lesson plans?

However, your approach is much more efficient and foolproof. No more messy guesswork! We need to step up and make bold strides toward safety!

Why stop at mobile devices and Pen Pal networks? I heard a student insult another student on Thursday. Perhaps it's time to ban speaking in school? I've noticed a ton of students disrupting class by blowing their noses. Is it time to ban tissues? Chair tipping has also become both disruptive and dangerous. When will we learn? Will it take a student's cracked skull to teach us to ban chairs?

At recess, I noticed students kicking balls around. One team refused to share the ball with the other team. Perhaps this is potential gang behavior? Bullying? Or maybe, like other schools throughout the nation, we just ban recess (or as I like to call it child-centered anarchy) altogether.

My issue is not with your banning of items, but with the fact that you have not gone far enough.

Sincerely:

Tom Johnson

Okay, I lied at the end. I wasn't all that sincere after all. Then again, I'm not sure they are all that sincere when they

CHAPTER SIX

speak of developing "holistic life-long learners." I decide at the last minute to avoid sending the letter. Perhaps I'm not all that different from those who suffer from Pencil Paranoia. Maybe I'm scared, too.

I'm struck by the fact that the real barrier to pencils is fear, not of the pencils, but of the freedom the medium offers. Thus, before I pen a letter to the district or speak out in a crowded pub, I have to recognize the same impulse in myself.

I have grandiose visions of how to change the educational system, starting with pencils and moving forward. If I'm not careful, I'm creating a new factory, thriving on new fears, stripping away the freedom to learn with or without a pencil.

*   *   *

The rainclouds gather and the class grows antsy in anticipation. For all the brick and concrete and steel of the school, the natural element has a way of awakening something primitive in everyone. It is not that the primitive is bad, either. It's simply deeper, more human, more earthy and real than dividing fractions.

The claps of thunder disrupt my monologue.

I let go.

Students gather near the windows and watch, studying first the drops and then the hail. A few brave souls venture outside and experiencing the pummeling of a lifetime, but the fist-fulls of atmospheric ice are a prize they relish.

"Is it safe to eat?" one asks.

PENCIL ME IN

A girl pulls out her paper and begins to draw. Her twin sister slaps her hand away and says, "Not yet. You can sketch later. Right now we can watch."

A boy standing by our class camera takes the twin's advice and sets down the machine. I'm not against banning tools, but on this rainy afternoon, it's clear that there is a time to abandon tools and embrace the natural world.

When we study conflict, we study Man versus Nature and Man versus Machine. Today, though, we are watching Nature versus Machine and though the war may be lost, this battle belongs to the clouds.

So, it leaves me with the realization that there is a time and a place to let go of the tools; to set down the camera, to drop the pencil, to crumple the paper, to disconnect the telegraph. But the goal should be restricting a medium in order to be freer, more human and more authentic. If we restrict tools out of a sense of fear, we are failing as a democracy. However, if we voluntarily set down our tools and embrace the grass beneath our feet, we are recovering what is lost under the industrial concrete.

CHAPTER SEVEN
Gray Matters

I visit two schools in our city that differ in their philosophy of pencil integration. The first is often touted as a state-of-the-art facility (it's more state-of-the-science, with hardly anything artistic about it) based upon a new Pencil Pedagogy. The second is a school that focuses on meaningful learning with pencils playing a secondary role.

In the first school, I notice a teacher talking through the entire lesson. She stands before the class with her Smart Chart, displaying pictures of the vocabulary. In another classroom, I watch the students use the self-paced Pencil Island program, where they complete a series of worksheets.

Indeed, in most classrooms I listen to teachers talk up the hardware hype, but few educators are willing to discuss actual teaching practice. "Look Techno-Tommy, check out these binders I'm using. You can drop one and it won't break. You can add tabs. They're amazing." So is student learning, but you wouldn't see it here. Most of the students in his class spend more time figuring out the binder than figuring out the math problems.

In another class, the teacher spends most of his time checking his mail pile while some of his students abandoned the school altogether to go catch a baseball game. When I point this out, he responds, "Look, they're safe. Besides, there's a lot of math in baseball. So I figure, let them go on their own field trip. When they come back they can add it to their pencil log. They should be able to go to any site they want. What's important is that they know how to find information wherever they go."

In the next school I visit, the teachers provide pencil-integrated instruction. Students use concept maps to plan out writing and create their shared documents. Those who struggle with the concepts can check out a tutorial binder. Teachers utilize the larger shared documents for brainstorming activities and students pass papers around during the editing phase.

In math class, they shift from slates to pencils and one teacher even allows students to use their own personal, miniature notebooks to take shorthand notes. They use manipulatives and mental math. They sketch examples of math within their context as the students construct their own learning.

When I ask teachers about their lessons, none of them focus on the pencils and paper. Instead, they share which strategies work best with which students. A teacher explains it this way, "Look, we like pencils. We just get more excited about learning. Some schools focus on pencil literacy. We focus on literacy."

Another teacher points out, "Our students begin school behind, because many of our students are still learning English. We differentiate between innovation and novelty. In most cases, novelty is a new toy. Innovation is a new way of thinking."

"What about the standardization of your school. It seems like you guys are doing the exact same, rigid curriculum," I ask.

"It seems that way, but it's horizontal, Tom. Our school lets us plan together and we have discussions about what strategies work best. Once we define the strategies then we talk about what tools to use. Sometimes it's slates and sometimes it's pencils. We have similar lessons, but we customize them to meet the needs of our students," she says.

"Don't you feel less autonomous?" I ask.

"Not at all. We're co-researchers. The teachers must document what is working in both qualitative and quantitative terms. Instead of fighting against an imposed curriculum, we're working toward shaping it," she explains.

"So, it's not the pencils?" I asked.

"I don't deny that the pencils have helped. But the power is in the way we think and not in the tools we use," she says.

Another teacher steps in, "Michelangelo wasn't a genius because he had the world's best chisel. It was his creative mind that made him a genius."

Paul the Preindustrial Poet talks to me afterward about it. "Tom, I think you were kind-of smug in your observations."

PENCIL ME IN

"What do you mean?" I ask.

"It was only a few months ago when your students nodded off in class while you were in front of a SmartChart and it was just this last summer when you raved about the need for a new twentieth century pedagogy," he says.

"I guess you're right," I admit.

"So, you figured out that progress for the sake of progress is useless. But there is still a danger in believing that your paradigm shift has now made you the ultimate expert," he says, clutching his pint.

"I guess I'm just worn out from the pencil hype. It's about the thinking process, not the tools," I say.

"If it's really all about the thinking, have you considered teaching a subject without any of the tools?" he says, shrugging his shoulders.

So the next day, I ask students to find the area of a volume of a cylinder that is twenty inches wide and twenty inches tall. I watch students fidget for a while before realizing that they need to solve this using a cerebrum rather than a slate or a paper.

No manipulatives.

No paper.

No slates.

No chalk.

Just a mind.

It takes awhile at first, but eventually every child answered it and then shares their process with partners.

CHAPTER SEVEN

Having tools is a part of being human. I never want to deny that. Yet, I also want to recognize that we have the power to abandon our tools and use our highly evolved minds. I ask students to do mental math because I want them to see that their brains are powerful in and of themselves.

*   *   *

It has me rethinking how I'm using pencils in my classroom. I'm struck by how often I simply find a pencil version of a slate exercise and nothing truly changes in my teaching. So, the students write a paper in pencil instead of ink. So, they use a plog instead of posting it on our class wall. The mental process doesn't change. What I want is critical thinking and creative thinking and deeper construction of knowledge. If technology can increase critical thinking, then it's transformative. Otherwise, it's simply a flashier version of slate-based learning.

Gertrude the CANDY LAND Specialist approaches me in mid-lesson to remind me of an emergency meeting. It's not really an emergency at all. No one has lost any limbs (though we will all lose a prep period).

"Your schedule says 'math block' right now and I see your students sketching pictures," she says.

"They're creating metaphors for the concept of 'x.' I want them to understand, on a deep level, what an independent and dependent variable mean and how they apply to life. So, they start with the picture and then describe the process using the metaphor."

PENCIL ME IN

"Look, I see kids drawing pictures of tools and bridges and revolutionary figures. Why not just teach them to define and use 'x' instead?"

"Metaphors are how we as humans make sense out of the abstract. It's the bridge between pure abstraction and the concrete, terrestrial reality we experience. It's used by children and philosophers alike to grapple with a complex universe," I say.

"I don't mind when you have the students replace the slates with paper, Tom. That's fine with me. I get it. They can go back and look at previous work. But this is a bit much," she says.

"Yes, but you miss the full potential of paper when we simply duplicate how we used it with slates. The genius of paper is how we can use it to construct knowledge rather simply copy processes."

"Your job is to teach them truth. Cold, hard reliable truth. Metaphors are messy and muddled and confusing - like a scavenger hunt through a swamp. It should be like clockwork. Mechanical. Bits and pieces as clear as day." I find it odd that she uses two or three metaphors herself to make sense out of his own theory of knowledge.

She walks to my desk and holds up a stack of concept maps. "What are these?"

"I had students do a quick concept map showing the relationship between linear equations, graphs, tables, functions and scenarios. I want to see them make the connection," I explain.

"So, use a vocabulary list," she suggests. "These are messy, Tom. Lines going everywhere. They look like refuse."

CHAPTER SEVEN

"What if learning is messy? What if confusion is the process that leads to clarity? What if simply memorizing a computational practice does little help students understand how a variable works?" I ask.

"Are you arguing that we should make math more confusing?"

"The world's greatest teachers were often confusing. Maybe, they understood that truth involves metaphors."

"Like whom?"

"Let's start with Locke, Rousseau, Plato, Erasmus, Jesus," I say.

"You aren't Jesus, Tom."

"I'm not claiming that at all. I'm simply pointing out that great teachers have always used metaphors," I point out.

"Look, it's just that metaphors are dangerous. There's too much room for confusion. I don't want you confusing our kids," she says.

"That's exactly why we need metaphors. Life is dangerous. Learning is dangerous. A bad metaphor can launch a war. I would rather have students use metaphors than become victims of metaphors that they don't understand. I want them to see that language shapes our perceptions of reality," I explain.

"How will this help them pass the test?" she asks.

"It's about thinking. If they think well about algebra, I have a hunch that they'll find the test easy," I suggest, though I have no evidence to back up this theory.

PENCIL ME IN

"I'm glad you have hunches, but our jobs are on the line with Caravan to the Top. Hunches and puppies and dandelions are all cute, but we have a test to pass. Okay?"

The real power of the pencil is that it becomes a symbol in our classroom. It's an unspoken reminder that learning always changes and that we sketch it out constantly, erasing misconceptions, refining previous thoughts, often delving in the paradoxical shades of gray. Yet, as long as we limit the thinking to simply "pass this test," we miss out on the power of the human mind.

*   *   *

"What are these doing here?" a student asks.

"Do we have to use those?" another student asks.

"Yeah, they're slates. You've used them, correct?"

"But this is a pencil classroom. We have paper. What are we doing with individual slates?"

I explain to my students that there are times when students will use paper and times they will use slates.

"But slates are so old school!" the student explains.

"True, but so is the human voice. Don't we still discuss things in class?" I point out.

"I thought you believed in the twentieth century classroom?" the student points out.

"I believe in learning. Ultimately, that's what it's all about," I respond.

"But I don't get it," another student point out. "We always use pencils."

CHAPTER SEVEN

"And that's the problem," I explain. "It's my fault. I should begin each lesson with the question, 'What do we need to learn?' and follow it up with 'What medium works best for this?' But oftentimes I go with the pencil and paper because it's the most convenient."

*　　*　　*

A few days later, the students begin their own Shakespearean production. I'd love a play by Henrik Ibsen, but he's too risky, suggesting that perhaps women are more than beautiful dolls. So, we work on *MacBeth*.

I'm secretly scared, wondering if maybe Gertrude has a point. Perhaps the pencils merely pacify the bored students. Perhaps the modern mind has outsourced the storing of knowledge to paper in order to move on to newer skills like analyzing and evaluating the information.

The students initially struggle with the need to memorize lines. "What if we just keep them in binders where we can search them later?" a child asks.

"We don't have to memorize the forty-five state capitols because you said it was a meaningless waste of time, right? So why memorize Shakespeare?"

"My goal is for you to think. When you memorize a capital, it's pointless. You will never show up to a state and instantly need to find the capitol. Unless you have the urgent need to meet with the governor, it's irrelevant. But Shakespeare is timeless. I ask you to memorize his work because it is meant to be meditated upon and spoken and acted out before an audience – even if the audience is only our classroom."

We don't abandon pencils as we approach a "traditional" unit. Instead, students write plogs and leave comments. I start a forum where they write short snippets on our wall. It's organized into threads where they can describe the themes of MacBeth, especially the danger of empty ambition. We use mind mapping to get a less linear idea of what everyone is thinking. In other words, we've moved from thinking about "pencil tools" to "mind tools."

*   *   *

Somewhere around Christmastime, they send the "pencil geeks" to a one-day workshop. I know it sounds cool, especially given the Yuletide connotations of the word. When I arrive, though, Paul the Preindustrial Poet informs me that we won't be making anything, even if it is a workshop. He passes out a few sheets of Buzzword Bingo to help pass the time.

I attend a workshop called "Paper for Creative Thinking." I assume that the workshop will include some science experiments or perhaps some ideas for problem-based learning. Instead, the speaker jumps out in a samurai costume and begins teaching us how to make origami cranes.

She explains to us how to follow the directions and transform a tiny square of paper into a crane. The directions are great and the crane looks interesting, but I keep hoping that this will lead into a deeper conception of creativity in the classroom. Instead, we move on to other animals, textures and colors.

CHAPTER SEVEN

Paul turns to me and says, "Origami is cool, but does it change the way we think about life?"

I overhear a woman ask him how this connected to learning and he responded, "The Japanese students continue to improve in their test scores. Some day they will beat us in achievement. Some say it is their curriculum, but I think it has to do with origami and its connection to creativity. A century from now, they will be creating automobiles that are the most reliable in the world and you will wish we had pursued 20th Century Origami Exercises."

I leave a positive evaluation, despite feeling disappointed. The speaker had passion, energy and a samurai costume to boot. However, I think she misunderstood something about paper and creativity. I could be wrong, but here's what I notice with my students: Creativity happens when people analyze problems, see things from multiple perspectives and develop a solution. Creativity happens when a student inquires about the world, develops a hypothesis and presents a new idea. Creativity occurs when a student conjures up a story or a poem or takes an unusual stance on a social issue. In other words, creativity doesn't have to look flashy. Creativity will happen when students have freedom and autonomy, when they find purpose in what they are doing and when they are not stuck in a system of rewards and punishments.

CHAPTER EIGHT
Solitary Confinement

Nong essentially networks together various social tools all within the confines of my classroom. I experiment with it not long before the winter break. The activity begins well. It is essentially like the Pen Pal networks with a few extra features. At first I need to redirect students who feel the need to decorate their space with all the colored pencils. Paul the Pre-Industrial Poet asks me if their misbehavior might actually be a creative learning experience.

"Perhaps in a world as black and white as slate and chalk, this is precisely what students need. Employers need creative thinkers."

Maybe Paul is right, but I doubt that employers are looking for workers who use Seymour Butts as a pseudo-name. I remind the entire class that we are not at home on Pen Pal networks and that this learning tool will be used for studying the Civil War.

CHAPTER EIGHT

After awhile, students catch on. A group in one corner joins a discussion zone, where they write their debate answers on threaded sentence strips. In another area, a group writes plogs and then leaves their comments in the margins. It's heated, but it's healthy.

On some level, I feel a sense of loss. For the first time ever, I am on the side rather than up front. Students work socially, find information independently and no longer feel the need to seek out the teacher as the source of knowledge. It's humbling. However, I quickly embrace the opportunity to work one-on-one and in small groups.

The next day is a nightmare. Apparently the Nong Network uses advertisements. The anti-industrial Populist in me cringes that a child's mind is being sold to marketing firms. Yet, I also see the value in learning tools. It's tricky. I tell myself it's okay to have a few ads, because there are advertisements all over the city. However, I don't have the same standards for other parts of the curriculum. Could you imagine an ad with Chester Arthur selling hair care products for those massive mutton chops right smack dab in the middle of a history book?

*   *   *

Apparently, a parent from the Temperance Movement believes her child will now become a full-scale alcoholic because of a beer ad.

The parent walks up to me and explains, "We're not keeping this under wraps. I called a socially conservative newspaper and they're running a story on this. It should hit the evening papers in a few hours."

PENCIL ME IN

"Okay, well I'm really sorry. I knew there were ads, but I had no idea one would involve alcohol."

"I need school to be a safe place for my child. I expect that." On some level, I get it. However, I think she's holding this to a different standard than she does the sites her son visits throughout his life.

The principal explains, "We understand your concern. We'll re-examine our policy about permitting ad-generated content."

"I'm worried about this pencil stuff. I got a set of colored pencils and some paper for my son. I thought he'd use it to learn. He joined this pen pal network and apparently he's writing letters to members of an organized crime syndicate."

"You're referring to mafia?" I ask.

She nods her head.

"It's a game. Just like the farm and sorority game." I explain.

"So, he's not thinking of joining a sorority either?"

"No."

"Still, I'm worried about exposing my son to the world so quickly and so young," she says.

"Hey, you wouldn't happen to have a newspaper with you right now?" I ask her. She hands me one.

"Let's see, the Lifestyle section. Look, an ad about meeting local singles. I'll check the sports section. Hey there's an ad for beer. Oh, and one for gin. And, if I'm not mistaken the Knickerbockers are playing in a stadium with beer advertisements as well. This is a real problem, considering your son idolizes athletes. What do you do to keep your child away from the newspaper?"

"Oh, I don't censor it. I mean, I want him to read. Sometimes we even read the paper as a family." The reality hits her and she moves from anger to embarrassment and she buries her face in her hands.

I look at her with a smug grin. I've won, or so it seems. Until she cries. Not simple tears, but huge sobs. She tells the story of her father being abusive when he was drunk and her former husband who would throw bottles at the kids when he had a few too many. Apparently, she left her entire life behind and moved to the city where she often sees drunk factory workers exposing her young daughter to a grown-up world and she wonders if the biggest danger isn't alcohol, but the fact that one of her children has to work 50 hours a week at the local factory for their family to survive.

Sometimes I get so focused on pencil integration that I miss the social reality that exists on a daily basis. Every child brings in a story and as a teacher, I have to make snap judgments based upon a sense of ethics that we may not all share. Teachers also bring in our own stories and often those stories clash and we fight to retain our voice and our character and a common setting.

The problem with these stories is that they're incomplete. And it leaves me wondering about the nature of social networks. What if she was right in being afraid, but her fear was directed at the wrong part of the social network? It seems to me the real danger is what I just experienced – the lack of context, the erasure of story and the sense that in this crowded social network nobody really knows anyone anymore.

The story never hits the evening papers. Was she bluffing or did she change her mind? Either way, I feel relieved. However, I'm also skeptical. What if she was right about exposing children to adult social situations too early? What if the real danger in a pencil world isn't the existence of pen pal predators, but the graying in the line between adult and child?

*　　　*　　　*

There are moments when I'm the one having a hard time adjusting to the collaborative nature of pencil-integrated learning. It's hard, for example, when I see what happens with social reading. "I hate when students underline their books with pencils," I complain to Mr. Brown.

"Why does it spark such a strong reaction? You're supposed to love pencils," he says.

"A page should be fresh each time one reads it. Let a student start with a pure page, free of the viewpoints of other readers. Whether you like it or not, reading is a solitary endeavor and I'd like to keep it that way," I say.

"Yes, but reading only became solitary with the advent of the printing press. Before that, when the resources were scarce, reading had to be social. So, people shared books, read books aloud, listened intently and spoke together. It has been a communal endeavor more often than individual," he reminds me.

"But we progressed toward individuality. Students now have access to books through our library. They share, but it's sharing on an individual level," I say.

"So, what if pencil is another form of progress? What if the pencil enables reading to be both social and individual? What if students can now read a book but also interact with it and share in an asynchronous dialog with past readers? What if they learn more from a book by the writing in the margins?" he asks.

"Or what if the social aspects of reading simply distract? What if they're too distracted by all forms of social media - from the loud phonograph to the emerging motion picture industry to the pen pal networks and the instant information on the telegraph? What if learning needs a little loneliness? What if solitude is good for the mind?"

We're at an impasse, both realizing that arguments are not games to be won, but neither of us humble enough to admit it. Mr. Brown doesn't know what to think of this anti-social rant. So we wait in silence and I finally ask, "Is that egg salad? It looks delicious."

"Yes," he says. "I'd share it with you, but eating should be a solitary endeavor."

*   *   *

Paul the Pre-industrial Poet tells me that I need to get onto a popular Pen Pal Network. He's an "early adopter," who tends to find technology quickly, explore it rapidly and then decide if he wants to keep it or dump it.

PENCIL ME IN

I tell him that his approach to technology reminds me of an uncouth bachelor who hasn't discovered the joy of marriage. He says, "I don't like your metaphor at all. I use technology, but it's because I don't want it to use me. I don't want to be married to a medium and forget about my real wife. So let's avoid human metaphors. The more we humanize the machine, the more we dehumanize ourselves."

"So, why should I join the pen pal network?" I ask.

"You need to be part of my PLN. It's how I connect with other educators. It's how I grow as a teacher," he says.

"Can't you just connect over a pint?" I ask.

"Does it have to be either/or?" he shrugs.

"I just don't see the big deal in using a pen pal network. I can't see the value in sending trite little messages to people on my free time," I say.

"So, if something is short, it's trite? What about parables and poetry and proverbs?" Paul is quite fond of alliteration.

"I just don't see what the big deal is with being on some kind of learning network," I explain.

"It's a social medium. You connect with people constantly and share ideas and resources and, on a good day, you share a part of yourself," he says.

"Every medium is social. I keep hearing this term 'social media,' but a letter is social. I send postcards all the time. Last time I checked, that's social. Front porches are social. It just seems to be a ton of hype," I respond.

CHAPTER EIGHT

"You might be right, Tom. But the only thing worse than creating unnecessary hype is the snobbery of avoiding a medium simply because people are excited about it," he says.

So I try it.

A few days after creating my own pen pal account, I listen in on a few students at lunchtime. They're talking about the pen pal networks.

"I only have twenty followers," a kid says.

"It's okay. Jesus only had twelve."

"That's not true. Jesus had thousands of followers. He just had his top twelve. He put them in his circle."

"True. So, maybe you're not Jesus. But I'm your friend and though I won't follow you around, I'll always pick you for shortstop even on your worst day."

I'm struck by the newfound fear that didn't exist when I was a kid. Or maybe it did. Maybe we were just as scared of social awkwardness, but we lacked a medium that would quantify our loser-ness in numerical terms. I didn't have a score telling me how little clout I had.

*   *   *

I receive a request from the insecure shortstop asking if I'd be his friend. I'm his coach, not his friend. So, I try my hardest to ignore it. However, as I think about my own childhood, I shudder. I can't imagine walking to kids' homes and seeing a list of friends. It would be like relational tryouts and I wouldn't have even made the junior varsity popularity team. I can't imagine what it would be like, in the formative years, when I was experimenting with how to interact with others, to have this massive public network of social relationships advertising to the world that I was a loser.

Still, it's not as if I can friend him. For what it's worth, I'd like to keep "friend" a noun rather than a verb. Can't a friend be the last refuge of permanence in an industrial world of change? We've already lost place and we're quickly losing thing. Let's keep our concept of person.

It's just that he and I can't be friends. I can't invite him with me to the pub and it would be downright creepy if I visited his tree house. I'm his teacher. He's my student. We aren't going to share stories about work or talk politics (and our shared anger at the McKinley administration for failing to deliver either hope or change in his Caravan to the Top initiative)

A few days go by before he stops me in class. "Why did you ignore my friend request?" he asks, calling me out on my act of passive-aggression.

"I'm sorry. You're my student and I just don't think we can be friends. Some day, when you're older, send me a friend request again, okay?"

He walks away, head hung low. He'll understand, right?

When I tell Mrs. Jackson about this, her response surprises me. "I would have accepted his invitation. I know there is a difference in age and I am concerned with the graying of adulthood and childhood in our country. It just seems like the last person to shun a child socially is a teacher. Socially awkward shortstop looks up to you."

"What about his parents?" I ask.

CHAPTER EIGHT

"I would have become their friends, too. I would have explained it all to them and talked about his need for a mentor. Besides, in the truest sense of the word, you are his friend," she explains.

"What do you mean?" I ask.

"A true friend is someone who looks out for others, who protects them and listens to them and ultimately that's what you are. Some day when he is an adult, you'll move from mentor to more of a horizontal friendship," she says.

So, I'm left perplexed. I set up rigid rules for social engagement and they seem to make sense to me. They are set up to protect myself from rumors. I don't want to seem like a creep. But in my goal to be safe, I've unintentionally crushed a kid.

Sketchy.

Gray.

I'm baffled by the subtle sense that the pencil-created world continues to transform social boundaries in perplexing ways. Ultimately, that's what makes pen pal networks so confusing. There's a lack of shared space. There's a confusion about social norms. I know when I go to church, it's safe to pray but not a great place to have a beer. I know it's okay to urinate in the woods but I'd be fired for doing that in school. It's this lack of true context that makes pencil-based collaboration both exciting and perplexing.

*   *   *

The district recognizes just how confusing these gray areas can be, so they form a committee on teacher-student community conduct. The district office human resource representative (are we really reduced to a resource?) explains the new Social Norms Proposal at the staff meeting, "From now on, teachers must avoid any site that allows for social networking with students."

"I can't believe this," Ms. Jackson says. "I . . . I've volunteered in my church's youth group for years. It seems that the best way to model appropriate adult behavior is to interact with kids and be a positive role model."

"No can do, Action Jackson! Churches can have creeps. Do we want you to seem like a creep?" he asks.

She shakes her head defiantly.

"What about the grocery store? I run into students at the grocery store all the time. It can be a real network of social interaction," Mr. Brown points out.

"Nope. You can be on the site, but you can't greet students. Just avoid eye contact and pretend that they don't exist. I mean, let's be honest, aren't you tired of the kids anyway?"

"I coach baseball," another teacher says.

"Is it the school's team?" he asks.

"No," he says.

"Then, you'll need to resign immediately," he says.

"I'm a family friend of one of my students. Her whole family has been over for dinner," a teacher explains.

"That might be misconstrued as a date. Just tell her family that you cannot be friends with them until their daughter is in college," he says.

"But she's in the fourth grade!"

CHAPTER EIGHT

"Well, they'll have to take a rain check, then. Any more questions?" he asks, surveying the room.

I raise my hand. "Can it be an anti-social networking site? I mean, can I go to a riot where my students might be attending? To me, that's pretty anti-social. Rioting is pretty anti-social," I add.

"Good point. We might need to revisit that. Let's go to the Board with this. Perhaps we'll simply pass a rule that you cannot interact with a student at all outside of school. Anti-social or social, it seems dangerous."

It seems to me that a better approach would include talking about the reality of community, the changes inherent due to the pen pal networks and the questions of how to interact socially in a way that is respectful and developmentally appropriate. Instead we go for uniformity and compliance.

*   *   *

I'm still trying to figure out the benefits of a pen pal network. My friends and family mostly send messages about make believe games where they pretend to run a farm. However, I begin to pursue the idea of Personal Learning Network more seriously. It's like a staff lounge without the bickering, gossip and complaining about children. We share ideas, pass notes and actually talk about teaching. It's like professional development without the annoying Edison Projector or the Kodak reps trying to convince me that their cameras will turn my students into geniuses.

I'm not suggesting that it's perfect. There is certainly this unhealthy desire within me to have people repost what I write so that I can feel more important. However, I'm not sure that it's the fault of the pen pal networks. I suppose it happens in any community. Call it sibling rivalry on a global level.

When a student overhears me talking about the PLN concept with Mr. Brown, she asks why students don't create their own PLNs. "It seems like that's the most natural way for students to learn," she adds.

So, we plan a unit that combines our plogs, shared documents, pen pal networks (I get permission to use Nong again) and mail in a problem-based learning activity. Back in the day it was considered cutting edge to send students on a "site quest" where they would do a scavenger hunt around the city. Now that seems quaint, contrived and almost cute.

The students examine an issue in their community and help develop a solution with the input of students around the world. Students participate with Paul the Preindustrial Poet's class and compare the perspectives from both sides of town. We run into structural issues, like schools that block pen pal networks and plogs. However, the project seems to lead to deeper dialogue regarding the problems and solutions in our community.

When the project ends, however, Paul's wife Gloria mentions to Ruth, "Paul would never say this, but his students were kind-of hurt. I know that none of the students meant it this way, but they treated his students as if they were second-class citizens."

Ruth wonders, "Is it possible that they treat pen pal collaboration as if it is all white noise? Just kind-of normal and culture-free."

CHAPTER EIGHT

"I think that's the problem. It's all noise and it's all white and for students of color that can feel pretty painful. Tom's students interacted according to their own cultural norms and they never even considered how that would marginalize Paul's class," Gloria points out.

It becomes a lesson on collaboration. Pencils can erase words, but they can't erase culture and conflict. Community will always be messy.

Gray matters.

*   *   *

I've grown to enjoy the Pen Pal Networks and I like the concept of growing my PLN. However, there are moments when I don't feel that I belong in here. By that I mean, I feel that I am a guest who snuck in the back door and people are too polite to tell me that I am being bombastic and rude when I think that I'm being honest.

For my part, I still have issues with the PLN concept. I often feel that we should be talking about the deeper human issues of education but conversation often feels like a party for pencils. In other words, people are spending their time on the pen pal networks writing about how great paper is and how it will revolutionize the education world. People swap stories of how amazing stationary days have been at school and wonder what it would look like if each child had a tablet in every classroom.

Subgroups of stamp collectors describe all the newest methods of sending letters and gush about how wonderful our socialized postal service is. People quote Edison on the disappearing role of the teacher in an age of electricity as if enlightenment comes from a filament in a bulb rather than the development of wisdom.

Paul the pre-industrial Poet puts it this way, "It's like throwing a party at my house where the honored guest is my house."

"Yeah, imagine a coffee shop where the main topic of conversation was coffee or visiting a house where the main conversation was the structural integrity of the tresses."

He smiles and adds, "Now imagine that this house had some really dangerous flaws and few people seemed to talk about it - the crowded capacity, the floor boards where people could easily slip through or the fact that so many people stayed inside the house that they missed the explosion of blossoms going on outside."

I don't mean this to be a criticism of my PLN. I do the same thing. I write little notes about how slow our telegraph can be at school or how nifty our cameras have become instrumental in student storytelling. But in the process, I miss out on what is really important. My students are telling amazing stories - pictures or not.

$$* \qquad * \qquad *$$

A student comes to me with a concern. "Mr. Johnson, I don't like the shared documents. I don't like the pen pal networks either."

"You don't like working in a group?" I ask her.

"No, I don't mind that. I just feel like when I write with a group and they add and subtract things from the document, it becomes some other thing that isn't my own. It's like I lose my personality or something," she says.

"I know what you mean. You lose your voice," I say.

CHAPTER EIGHT

"Yeah, and it doesn't always feel safe to write something that goes completely against what the group thinks. Especially when they are strangers," she says.

Another student mentions to me her concern about the lack of privacy. "I find myself thinking way too hard before I write one of those 140-character messages. I miss being able to just tell someone something from across the classroom. And it's like it stays forever on the pen pal network. It's like it's permanent."

Her friend adds, "Sometimes I feel like I'm making up this whole separate person that interacts on the pen pal networks and I can't figure out if the physical me or the pencil me is the real me. I sometimes spend so much time on this public pencil self and I wonder if I'm letting my private self die."

Die? Really? Eighth graders can be quite dramatic. And yet I see where she's coming from. No one told me that people would write personal notes on my wall or stick photographs of me in public spaces. It's not that I want to hide, per se. It's just that I'm not sure a photo of me at the Haymarket Square riot will look good in front of the school board. I never thought in advance the reality that the vapor-self, the ever-evolving imago would be amplified. I feel a bit like a celebrity and it feels both gratifying and terrifying at the same time.

Ultimately what we gain in collaboration is a connection to others. This web of connections becomes our safety net but also a spider web. We gain meaningful interactions with others, but we lose solitude – the loss of a voice, the loss of privacy and on some level, the loss of self.

In losing the sense of self, though, we also lose our sense of space and time and community. A PLN cannot be a community. A social network cannot replace a stoop. Want some real collaboration? Ed has a decent chat each week on his social network (apparently thousands of people show up to Ed Chat), but I also enjoy the local café. I fear that, as we erase the sense of space and time and self, we lose out humanity. We lose our community. Yes, it's transformed. But it's also lost. Forever.

*   *   *

I share these thoughts over a pint with Paul the Preindustrial Poet.

"I worry that, in an industrial world, we might become so immense that we become myopic," I explain.

"I see what you mean," he says.

"Like it's the Emperor's New Clothes and we're expanding this empire and failing to see our own nakedness. Don't get me wrong, we can go on about Manifest Destiny, but if cheap goods and more factory is our vision of humanity, I begin to doubt progress. We're being innovative. We're trying the Next Best Thing. We're moving forward . . ."

". . . but no one seems to be asking where we are going," he says.

"I started this journey with the goal to create the Next Big Thing. I had a vision of a pencil-based curriculum. I soon ran into the political, social and relational barriers and recognized that I didn't have all the answers. From there, I realized that the real power is not so much the tools as the thinking. And now I'm recognizing that I was wrong again. Technology is dangerous."

"I think that's the journey, though. You were a foreigner and you became a tourist. You caught a glimpse of it and you became an immigrant," he says.

"And now I'm a citizen? A citizen who thinks critical about pencil land," I say.

"Technology might be a tool, but we are kidding when we believe we can predict its effects on us. But as much as we shape the tool, the tool also shapes us."

"Sounds a bit like animism," I say.

"Perhaps. And maybe it's dangerous to deny its magic," he says.

"It's humbling," I lament.

"It is evidence of human hubris to believe that we have ultimate control over how a medium changes human interaction."

"That's it! It always dehumanizes. Technology is so often inhuman. Our communities, our relationships, everything. It's becoming less human."

"Maybe. But creating and using tools is a deeply human endeavor. We can't deny that any medium, including the human voice, can be harmful. Simply saying 'this tool is good' or 'this tool is bad' or even 'let's make sure we use it only for good' denies the deeply human relationship with have with our tools. The relationship is always more complicated and more powerful than simply claiming we can use it the right way."

"So, what's the solution? I can't simply teach kids to be critical of a medium and assume they are the experts who will use it wisely," I point out.

"But you can teach them to question the technology around them. You can ask them to be humble. Being a tech expert, even a Luddite expert, won't inhibit the hubris. Only humility can change that."

*   *   *

I held my daughter the other night and she could hardly see the stars. I think that gas lamps in the street are a grave mistake. We traded in our connection to the cosmos for a little false security. So, I can see a street thug, but I miss the vast universe that surrounds me.

If the magi lived in our urban enclave, they would have missed the incarnation. Sometimes I wonder if the same happens here. We sacrificed all things deep and human and spiritual in our drive to create a technocratic paradise. We can't see the divine.

Tonight I'm lost.

It's hard to see the universe when surrounded by smoke stacks.

CHAPTER NINE
Losing Our Voice

With the popularity of *The Voice Collective* and the professional development workshops that the district had me conduct, I find myself thrown into the position of Chief Pencil Guru. It's nothing formal, but I get a shot at using additional technology sponsored by Robber Barons like and Andrew Carnegie and Thomas Edison.

"Don't do it," Paul warns me in late January.

"It's a shot at technology tools that I had never dreamed I would have in my classroom," I explain.

"Who owns those tools?" he asks.

"They're a gift," I explain.

"A Trojan Horse," he adds.

"They belong to the school. It's not like Carnegie is hiring me to work for him," I explain.

"But it's moving toward the corporate ownership of a civic institution," he says. "Think about how you started. Pencils and papers donated locally. You're losing something here."

The words sting. I want him to be happy for me.

*   *   *

Initially, I assume that the acceptance of my proposal would transform my status within the school. I wouldn't have to fight the small battles over when the students can access a technology tool.

However, as I walk into my classroom with the brand-new phonograph, a man from the district stops me. "Yeah, um, this is blocked. Sorry dude, but you can't have your students use the phonograph."

"Why is that?"

"Well, it could have dirty words. After all, these are Victorian Times. Who wants to risk a lawsuit?"

"I see your point, but students could also speak a dirty word as well. So, I don't really see why a change in the medium is all that different."

His boss walks up to me. "Techno-Tommy, it's not about that at all. It's about our limited capacity for music. See, the school band will be using this hallway and they need it for their classroom. It's just not that wide. We can't fit all the instruments and fit a phonograph. So, with limited band-width, we have to either block the phonograph or slow everybody down."

"Why can't we just use a different hallway or perhaps build a new one?" I ask.

"I don't know. I'm just the IT guy," he says.

"The what?" I ask.

"I'm an Instrument Technician. If you have issue with this, talk to the district," he says.

"So, I get to have this great new technology, but I'm limited because of band width?" I ask. He shakes his head.

I find a way to sneak the phonograph in through the back door. I just think it's sad that we have to find back door methods of accessing tools that will be useful for learning.

*   *   *

We begin the unit using the phonograph just as Edison intended it – as a dictation device in a corporate setting. I plan out a unit that mirrors "the real world" and students must run the classroom as an efficient office where they do jobs that mirror their future career ambitions. Mrs. Jackson thinks this is a bad idea. She reminds me that they are eighth graders and asking them to choose a future career is insane when they cannot legally drink or get married or join the military.

"But I want it to be like the real world," I explain.

"You say this as though your classroom is a fantasy land inhabited by drunken wood gnomes and fire breathing dragons and sprites who steal your coffee when you're not looking. Please, Tom, your class is already real. The business world, however, is often artificial. Why push that on them now?"

"Mr. Johnson, why do we use phonographs?" Cynical Gifted Boy asks.

"It's a learning tool. Why do we learn?" I ask him.

PENCIL ME IN

"We learn to pass the test so that we can pass the test to get into the honor's program in high school so that by 1901 we can pass the new SAT test so that we can get into the better university so that we can get a better job," Cynical Gifted Boy answers.

"What then?" I ask him.

"I think you work really hard doing what you hate and look forward to retirement, where you wonder what happened to your life and why no one wants to talk to you, because they are too busy passing the test to get the job to get the high pay to guarantee that they'll have a good retirement. Then you die lonely and people say nice stuff about you when you aren't around to hear it."

What if we taught in the now rather than as a preparation for the future? Don't get me wrong, we are always preparing for something else, but it happens by being relevant today. Students should use pencils and paper, not because it is necessary for a particular job, but because it is what they need right now to learn.

It has me wondering if the real price tag on the phonograph is in the purpose of education. When I receive a professional-grade tool, I now feel the need to justify it and to get my money's worth. There is an unspoken pressure to make it productive and the minute education becomes an issue of productivity is the moment it becomes an economic commodity. Perhaps Paul is right. Maybe this is a Trojan Horse.

* * *

Later that week, a man rides his carriage up to the playground. He pulls out a hand-cranked, ultra-portable, larger-than-the-cosmos phonograph. The song is not a pretty piece by any means. Far from

Mozart, it is a repetitive drumbeat and a song with some choice words that the average primary grade student doesn't use (Indeed, it was a bit of a shock to the kindergarten class whose idea of "dirty language" includes poopy face and stupid head).

I suppose his main goal involved impressing five and six year olds, not by creating his own innovative music, but by blasting a record loud enough for everyone to hear. A student points out to me, "Knowing how to use technology doesn't mean you know how to use it."

I ask the students to set down their pencils and discuss the question, "What does it mean to know how to use a medium?" From here, we discuss the loss of silence in our world, the humming sounds of industry and the choking clouds of soot from the factories.

"So, I can do more, but I'm so rushed that I don't have time to do anything," a girl explains.

"Everything is compressed," a kid says. "We pack more into it, but we lose the quality."

"Can you elaborate on that?" I ask.

"I can take a picture and it's portable, right? But it's not as good as a painting. I can listen to music on a phonograph, but it's all scratchy. We have some motion pictures, but they're choppy. People are now eating canned meat and it's processed and has the texture of jelly."

I want my students to be geeks and gurus. The geek is knowledgeable about technology. This person loves it, embraces it and knows how to use it in creative ways. One the best days, the geek thinks of the future and how technology can be used to solve social, economic and perhaps even personal problems. On the worst days, the geek becomes intoxicated by the novelty and applies futuristic solutions that lack foresight. Or, the geek is simply a guy on a wagon with a really loud phonograph, imposing his narcissistic desires on the world.

On the other hand, the guru is wise about technology. This person sees it as a force that is sometimes negative in its dehumanizing aspects. On the best days, a guru will remind us that the physical is as important as the mechanical and that some things in life should not be chopped into pieces, processed, compressed and industrialized. A guru knows that, even when we try and predict it, technology takes on a life of its own. However, on the worst days, a guru will grow cynical and angry and shake an elitist fist at every innovation while missing out on the ways technology improves society.

I want my students to be a bit of both. Call it a paradox or a mystery or a contradiction. I don't want them to abandon technology in a doom-and-gloom fear. However, I also don't want them to get into the mentality that a robotic world will fix everything.

*   *   *

Every so often this guy named Ted likes to gather around the world's movers and shakers to offer short lectures on the "visions of the twentieth century." I know it sounds a little bit like a cult, but these aren't magical mind readers. They don't sacrifice animals to the industrial gods or read tea leafs or anything. Most of them are geeks like me, just smarter and with more money, influence and power.

So Ted invites my class to visit the latest Ted Talk. Because of our work with the phonograph and pencils, he assumes we will be intrigued by the great intellectual movers and shakers.

A student points out to me, "Isn't that Andrew Carnegie?"

"It looks like it is," I say.

"I can't believe he is lecturing us on what it means to be a philanthropic citizen. I enjoy our library, but I have an uncle who worked in one of his steel mills. When the machine chopped off his arm, the company did nothing."

I sit uncomfortably through the talk with the image of a bloody appendage hanging from a steel worker. Apparently acquiring a massive amount of wealth through the use of monopolistic endeavors gives a man moral authority over others. I whisper to the boy, "Having free books isn't that great of a privilege when you have lost your eyesight in the steel mill." He nods his head in agreement.

Next is a man named Phil Bates. He seemed like a nice guy, slightly fidgety and a little shaky, but he seems nice enough. Bates first talked about the need to fix all of the poverty in Africa. It has a slight tone of "white man's burden" to it, especially considering the fact that he failed to address the larger issues of continental poverty due to colonialism and imperialism.

He then moves into teacher-bashing mode and talks of the need for more professional teachers following the scientifically proven best practices. The speech offends me for a few reasons.

Phil Bates never finished college and he wasn't a great student, either. The man has no formal knowledge about the educational system, no registered research to back up his claims and no peer-reviewed articles under his name. Sure, he gives away some free paper. However, it does not seem like charity to offer your paper products at a discount. It is product dumping. Telling kids they "need it" because "that's what businesses use" only stifles future pencil innovations and ensure that his company has a greater market share in the future. Furthermore, the assumption that schools only exist to serve private industry goes against the very notion of public education and the original intent of developing critical thinking citizens.

I'm struck by the reality that this is the same process as the Phonograph Man, except the carriage is nicer and the phonograph fancier and the music is playing something more corporate. But I've wasted half a quarter teaching my students how to dance to somebody else's music.

So, I rethink the whole phonograph concept and have students create their own recordings based upon the local history of the area.

We meet a few former Civil War veterans who talk about the human side of a Total War. Students interview women of the era who offer a perspective that the textbook is unable to present, because, like the Phonograph Man, the textbook company is in love with their own loud, male-only voice. The people we interview begin referring us to others in the community who share their own voices. The result is a live chorus that cannot be captured by a phonograph. Sure, students use the technology and write about it with the pencils, but the learning is live.

$$*\qquad *\qquad *$$

As we shift into an industrial age, it seems that we are more intimate than ever with technology. While one used to spend the day connected to the land, toiling in hopes for a better crop, we now spend the days connected to the assembly line, a mere cog in the machinery. We're losing our voice.

With that in mind, I have students write letters to personified technology. At first, the class is skeptical, but over time they warm up to the idea. Many of them chose to write multiple letters. While we have analyzed media before, the personal tone of a friendly letter pushes my students to think deeper about the human side of technology in society.

Dear Automobile,
    You will never replace the horse. Although you might be faster, I can't imagine that mankind will choose convenience over relationships. We know our horses. We don't know our horseless carriages. Besides, our city might be crowded, but where would you possibly need to go that you couldn't access on horseback?
Sincerely,
Mildred

Dear Light Bulb,
    You have replaced the sun in providing warmth and illumination. Your small filament might be weak, but you have already managed to fade our sense of seasons. I stood outside last night and stared at the stars and the universe felt small and manageable. Although I appreciate you, I wish you would take a few nights off so that I could have an evening of awe.
Sincerely,
Robert

PENCIL ME IN

Dear Telegraph,
   Maybe I am too hopeful, but I think you have the ability to spread information instantly around the world. I'm hoping we can have a more democratic world. Perhaps there is something we can learn from other countries and they can learn from us.
                    Sincerely,
                    Sarah

Sometimes I miss the days of technophilia. I miss the grandiose visions of a New 20th Century Education. (Always a proper noun. Very important) After pushing toward pencil integration, I'm seeing how it redefines our identity and our voice and our social interactions. It's exciting and it's scary.

It's also profitable.

I don't want my students to become a cog in a educational machine. I don't want them to sell their minds for a set of phonographs and some flashy new tablets. Yet, I also want my students to master the medium and understand how to share their voice in a respectful, critical thinking way.

So, where's the middle ground? Where is that comfortable place of moderation? It doesn't exist. Instead, we remain in a constant flux, in a state of paradox, pulled by two different forces, the geek and the guru, and all the while trying to figure out how to speak and to listen in a sketchy world.

CHAPTER TEN
Capturing Life

With the shipment of the seven cameras, I initially plan to launch into instructions regarding proper use. However, my newfound Luddite streak forces me to ask the students to think about the medium first. I ask them to write a plog post answering the question, "What holds more power: words or pictures?" To my surprise, the students do not all agree. I assume that with the novelty of the photograph, students would write about picture power.

"A picture can tell you what is empirically real while words can write about reality that we cannot express in a photographic form. Show me a picture of love. Show me a picture of hope," a student writes.

Another simply writes, "I like pictures better. They're easier to understand." Every child is at a different place in tech criticism.

One student writes, "Photographs are more permanent. They are more objective. They capture the truth without having to be reinterpreted. There are less layers of communication to go through. You can't edit a picture."

Another student disagrees, "Pictures are more emotional and more subjective. It's because there are no words. There is no context. The photographer has deliberately framed a scene, just one scene, and you're stuck with it."

I begin with this concept of move powerful and we more into: Which captures reality better? Which captures the truth better? Most students tend to believe that a person can change words, but that pictures are un-doctored. So, I show them the famous Lincoln picture with the body of John Calhoun. They're floored.

"How'd they do it?"

"Photo editing. They just brought it to the photo shop and copied and pasted, I guess."

"Wow, so photo shopping can alter our view of history," a boy says.

A girl asks, "How do you know what's real if you can just manufacture truth by changing pictures?"

"Isn't that what we do with words?" a boy asks.

"What if all truth is manufactured? We keep asking 'does the photograph capture truth' and it's not something out there that we capture. It's something we make up as we go along," a student points out.

CHAPTER TEN

*　　　*　　　*

The students work on a project called "camera-captured conflict and compromise in context." I pride myself on the alliteration, though I spend a longer time defining the vocabulary than I had assumed. I also take about an hour to go over how to use camera. Apparently Pencil Natives aren't Camera Natives. For all the talk of a "multimedia generation," students have never heard of the Rule of Thirds and hardly grasp the concept of lighting.

I stop by a table where the documents remain blank and the students simply talk to one another. One boy says, "I left my notebook at home." Another one explains, "I'm talking about the project with my classmates and I'll do the pencil work at home."

Table after table, I experience the same trend: students playing with the camera or obsessing over the novelty and missing the learning. "Can't you figure it out? It's not about the technology? It's not about the tools. It's about conflict and compromise." I spout off a string of sarcastic remarks and slowly move from yelling to screaming.

Kids are scared.

One student takes a picture. The flash snaps me out of it.

*　　　*　　　*

"You can use this if you want," I tell him later in the day. It's the awkward time of pulling out shrapnel from my explosion. The students are gracious in accepting my apology, but I still teach with a limp.

"I won't show it to everyone. But I have a plan for it."

PENCIL ME IN

He develops it in the dark room and then writes a narrative about anger and silence and the ways in which he forgets that his behavior can set off adults. It streams from prose to poetry almost flawlessly.

I stare at the photograph and remark, "This really captures life, doesn't it?"

So, I write the following letter, not in pencil, but in pen. I want it to be permanent.

Dear Students,

My words were hurtful. My tone was mean. I grew angry and I lost it. As the adult in the classroom, this is inexcusable. I'm really sorry. I don't want this to define me. I don't want this to become my style of interacting with you.

When I first got the cameras, teachers warned me that students would all of a sudden be "off task." See, in our profession, we have this magical formula called Time on Task and it helps determine if students will be successful in their education. I scoffed when I heard that projects and pencils and pictures would all take my students "off task."

However, I watched as you moved off-task. I saw daydreaming. I heard conversation that seemed "off task." I noticed some of you pulling away from your project for a while. Was I providing too much freedom? Was this a failed experiment? When I corrected you, a few of you commented, "I'm working on this part at home," or "just let me think." I assumed you were being disrespectful and I reprimanded you verbally and publicly.

When I saw the finished products and participated in the conversations, I noticed how deeply you had been thinking. It hit me: it's not about being "on task" so much as it is "thinking deeply." It's not about work completion, because learning is not a chore. You taught me that if students are excited about learning, they will end up working harder.

So, again, I'm sorry. I don't mean this to be an excuse for a class of anarchy. I'm just saying that from now on, I am going to focus less on what you do and more on what you are learning.

CHAPTER TEN

Sincerely,
Mr. Johnson

*   *   *

A few days later, the candid camera boy comes up to me and says, "Do you remember what you said about the camera capturing life?"

"Yeah, I remember that," I say.

"Well, I don't think life should be captured. It should be lived. You can take a picture like that and it doesn't tell the whole story. It's just a slice of life and I'm thinking that life shouldn't be all sliced up like that. It's not a carrot."

"I see your point," I say.

"It makes me wonder about the world created by images. You know, you are a good teacher. But people could see that one picture all out of context and it would send the message that you are a jerk," he explains.

"Maybe we're all capable of being jerks," I add.

"Yes, but in the course of a lifetime we get a bigger picture of events and words and actions. The photograph is limited to a split second. I think that's dangerous. Maybe that's the down side of photographs," he says.

"I agree that it's dangerous. You know, people act different when they know they are on camera. They get all serious. People might see a photo album from our age and think we never smiled. I think that shapes people in ways we don't realize," I respond.

My goal is to teach students to criticize the tools they use and to use the tools they criticize. When I phrase it the first way, I feel like a renegade. When I phrase it the second way, I feel like a hypocrite. Language shapes reality and we're moving to a world where language is imagery. Words are replaced with pictures and if Edison has his way, we will live in a world of streaming motion pictures. If you can manipulate imagery, you can have people's minds.

I want students to make sense out of the image-based world. I want them to be media critics. I want them to know that life, real life, cannot be captured on a photograph. And yet, I also want them to see the beauty of photography in its ability to tell a story. The medium is dangerous. Not good or bad, but powerful.

*   *   *

A few months back, I wrote a long proposal about changing our school into a 20th Century School. I used buzzwords and jargon and research that never really made much sense to me. I avoid the confusion and ambiguity that I feel when students take pictures and instead describe how "a multimedia platform will help develop creative leaders for the twentieth century."

One of the judges for this large education grant pulls me aside, "Would you share your story of pencil integration?"

"I guess it's a bit of a love story," I respond.

He furrows his eyebrows and strokes his handlebar mustache. "I'm not seeing your point entirely."

"You know it's a bit trite, I suppose. I fell in love with pencils. I mean, I thought I knew pencils. I could talk about the feel of a pencil in my hands and the moment of excitement when I first scribble some words. But I think I was in love with the idea of pencils. I mean, it was the notion of writing and editing my words - the idea of it - not the act itself that I loved."

"I'm not sure I'm understanding it one bit," he answered.

"I do this with all technology, I guess. I fall in love with it before I know it. Then I see a dark side and I run. For me, with pencils it was the notion of the temporary side of pencils that scared me. It was the question about sloppiness. I love to write, but I was afraid I would be too casual and my writing would decline."

"And . . ." he says in frustration.

"So I got critical of pencils for a few months. I started seeing only the bad side of it. Then I decided that I love pencils. I love the writing and editing process, the shading and smudging of pencil art, the feel of a notebook and the marks on my hand. I love the power of a temporary medium - the notion that all could be erased at any moment. 'Pencil me in' isn't as permanent as 'having ink done.' Seriously, would anyone ever have a pencil tattoo?"

"I'm not sure where you're getting at," he says.

"See, so much of my life is permanent. And that's good. Marriage, family, my profession. I love the permanence of that. But pencils are constantly changing. And I fell in love with them for the very temporary nature of it all. It was the classic boy meets pencil, boy throws all pencils away and then boy comes back to pencils forever narrative," I say.

He looks at me in silence and shakes his head.

"See, I fell in love blindly, saw the dark side, hated pencils and then came back with a love that recognizes the critical side of pencils. Does that make any sense?" I ask.

He shifts awkwardly and asks, "Can you explain how this relates to your immediate classroom?"

"My students are taking pictures of conflict and compromise," I tell him.

"Ooh, that's wonderful," the man says.

"Yeah, it starts out with students being infatuated with photography even thought they know nothing about the art."

"You mean science," he says.

"Sure. But we also talk about the danger of capturing life and we debate whether or not words are more powerful and more accurate and more authentic than pictures. I'm not sure if it's true that some tribes believe that the camera can take one's soul, but I suppose that was our internal monologue. So, we fell in love with pictures, but it was a tumultuous love story. I think the conflict allowed the love to be real," I say.

"So you don't like technology?" he asks.

"No, I love it. I love phonographs and photographs and pencils, but I love it realistically. It's not a blind love," I respond. "That's my whole point. You wanted a story. Well, that's our story. That's been the process, the journey, the storyline," I say.

The grant man stares at me blankly and says "thank you," though I don't really think he meant it at all. I imagine he will tell his colleagues, "I simply wanted to know how he uses pencils in his classroom. I need to know that he'll use our money wisely and he gets into this strange esoteric metaphorical quasi-Luddite, strangely technocratic rant about loving media."

*   *   *

CHAPTER TEN

"Mr. Johnson, do you think people will confuse us when we're gone?" a student asks.

"What do you mean?" I ask.

"I mean, when we're all dead, will people look at the pictures and get the wrong picture?" Kids say some of the most confusing and morbid things.

"I'm still not seeing your point," I respond.

"I mean, after we're dead and our children are dead. Generations from now, will people look back at the scowls on our faces and think that things were more serious back in the day? I mean, will they think kids never threw a paper or slammed a slate down or smiled when they hit a home run or told a joke? Will the picture be telling a lie?"

"All my pictures have this ridiculous, serious look," a gregarious girl points out. "It isn't me at all."

I stop the class at this point as we discuss what we record, the artifacts we leave behind and the huge gaps that are missing in history as a result. It has me thinking that maybe that's the tragedy of technology and the pitfall of posterity. It always leads to selective memory.

*   *   *

Imagination.

Imaginary.

Root word: Image.

Imago.

Make believe.

Make belief.

PENCIL ME IN

We are living in a world just beginning to shift from a print to an image culture. We create imagery. No, we capture imagery, letting imagination believe it is less important or less real or less true than the flash of a camera.

But we also create images; spinning truth and reality to improve the image we try and maintain with the vain hope of masking our mortality.

Graven images.

I spent an hour retouching a photograph I'll use in my pen pal network. It might capture reality, but I feel less real than I did an hour before when I broke bread with my wife and daughter. (Okay, I had to break the bread into really tiny pieces for her, but it was still breaking bread) When I share the sense of confusion in sketching out a pencil-based image of myself, my wife reminds me that it is human.

Ruth warns me, "Tom, we hide. We stay out in the open. We hide again. Social context, language, clothing - these are all a part of the natural desire to create that element of self that we experience so deeply."

"It just seems like we lost something human in the process," I say.

"No, our technology, our tools, our language, culture . . . those are what make us human. The need to develop an image is the root of imagination. It's what makes us who we are. It's pictographs on cave walls and hieroglyphics on pyramids and stained glass on cathedral walls. The tools might change, but the sense in which we create an image or capture an image and then call it reality . . . that is a part of what makes us human," she responds.

My daughter paints a monster. It's real, or at least it is real to her. I retouch a photograph. My wife quilts a blanket. True, we might be moving toward an "image culture." However, let's not kid ourselves. We have always been image-based. It's just that the tools change in how we express imagination. Yet, whether we conjure up a new vision or try and rethink our public memory, it is always an act of imagination.

Imagination.

Image.

Imago.

"Imago Dei," she reminds me as I slowly slide the air shudder and watch the silhouettes fade into darkness. Even now, as I embrace her beneath our comforter, I am experience at once the empirical reality of her warmth and conjuring up images of that moment she walked down the aisle. Even when we are laid bare, in our most vulnerable moments, we are still bound by our images.

The next morning, I notice my four-year old daughter sucking in her stomach in front of the mirror. She glances at the huge billboard of the tiny-waisted woman in the corset and then back at herself. Her concept of reality is based on the image culture around her. Might as well be a Word Wall spelling out in bold letters, "Your self worth is based upon how your waistline measures up. Your image is your identity."

CHAPTER ELEVEN
Life on a Graph

I meet up with Paul the Pre-industrial Poet. It's an early spring day, so we meet outside for our weekly pint. Food tastes better outside. I'm sure there's a technology metaphor in there somewhere.

"So, I met with the sales guy from the American Telephone and Telegraph Company. He's trying to sell me on this idea of having a telephone in my room and a telegraph at my school."

"Are you going to do it?" he asks.

"I have my reservations. It just seems like another example of a teacher-centered technology. Like an Edison projector or a chalkboard from Man-Who-Stole-Fire-From-The-Gods company.

Seriously, a century from now every classroom will have a phone and teachers will still be the ones to use it."

"Maybe. Or a century from now, they'll find a way to combine the telephone and the telegraph and they'll make it portable. It's what happens to all media. Pictographs are permanent and expensive and located on cave walls and then they are portable on papyrus and then the printing press turns reading from a collective experience to an individual one. Some day they'll do the same to motion pictures and telephones and telegraphs all on the same device."

"Sounds cool to me. Students will finally have a chance to use a technology that was once teacher-centered. In another century students will have all the tools at their fingertips. Schools will have to embrace it," I say.

"I doubt it. Schools will ban them, because the real issue is one of power. Who wants students to have instant access to information at all times? Dangerous stuff, Tom. Teachers won't want to give up the control. So, my guess is that like the pen pal networks and the personal journals, schools will ban the portable telegraphs."

"So should I go with it?" I ask him.

He evades the question. "I think the real danger is the supplier. Look, you keep trying new technology. You've gone beyond the pencil and that's great, Tom, but I wonder what the cost is."

"It's been free so far," I add.

"And if you get the grant you wrote, it will continue to seem free. But it comes with strings attached. There's always strings attached. Even if the telegraph went wireless, there would still be strings attached. Companies don't just give you technology. They buy it with an agenda," he says.

"So, what's the agenda?" I ask.

"Profit," he says.

"Well, maybe we all profit. Maybe my students profit from having a state-of-the-art education and the corporations profit financially," I respond.

"I hope you're right," he says shaking his head.

*   *   *

The project turns out to be more extensive than I had imagined, with the use of both the telegraph and the telephone. The students do a "virtual" book club with students in another large city within the state. Within this project, they send short telegraph messages and make phone calls about the Elements of Literature.

I know that I am already past the stage of "integrating" technology. The goal is now to think critically about the technology that one uses. However, unlike the photography project, this one feels clunky, as if we are trying to fit the learning into the telegraph rather than using it naturally as we go.

A student has an idea for a more authentic method. "Mr. Johnson, what if we used the telegraph and telephone in the same way that reporters do?"

"Describe what you're thinking."

"Well, we could actually go out and report about some of the themes of our books."

So, the students get contact information and make phone calls. One group is reading a rather preachy contemporary Dickens novel, so they contact a local charity and interview the founder. From there, they use the phone to solicit supplies and start their own service project. Another group, after reading The Red Badge of Courage, makes phone calls to a former Civil War soldiers who then come in for a phonograph session. It's chaotic for me. I have a hard time letting go. Yet, it's part of the pencil mentality – the notion that learning can be flexible.

*   *   *

Gertrude pulls me aside late in the third quarter and says, "I know you have been using pencils this year, but you're not planning to let them use erasers on the assessments are you?"

"I think it's a great tool. Students can erase mistakes as they go or they can erase them after the fact."

"Yes, but how do you have common assessments if you don't have common methods of assessing?"

"I'm not sure I see your point," I add.

"Well, a kid can just erase his or her work at any given point," she says.

"Isn't that what learning is all about? What about our slogans of life-long learning? What about our vision statement of loving learning? Those don't count anymore?"

She launches into a long lecture about formative and summative assessment and I tune her out. It's a small battle to fight and I nod my head and pretend to care. I'm not changing my approach. See, if pencils and erasures represent anything good, it is the notion that one can always change. Growth is always possible. Learning is not a fixed commodity, but a journey.

"How will you grade their work if they can just go back and change things?" she asks.

"I don't grade it. They do portfolios."

"Doesn't that make kids lazy?" she asks.

"Not at all. They work harder because I take away the bribes and extortion. I can't claim to support the notion of developing democratic citizens and go with a totalitarian style of assessment."

The conversation ends with a long lecture on the Bell Curve. We finally "agree to disagree" which is a nice way of saying, "we'll just choose to casually ignore one another."

She finally ends with, "All your cuddly bunny coddling is doing a disservice to them. It's not how the real world operates." Perhaps. But I have a hunch that in the real world they just might use pencils.

*   *   *

Midway through the project, I ask students what they think of communicating via telephone.

"I think it's better," a girl explains. "We aren't confined by our own classroom walls. We can go anywhere that the operator allows. It's like being two places at once."

"I don't know how I feel about that. I don't always feel present when I'm physically here. I wonder if it's a good thing to let my voice travel over the wires and into some other place. I'm not sure we're meant to be that way," a girl adds. "Maybe we were meant to be *here,*" she says, gesturing around the classroom.

CHAPTER ELEVEN

"I find myself making gestures at the phone. It's like I forget that our interaction isn't real. I mean, I could stick my middle finger out and the other person wouldn't see it," a student explains.

"It's not real. I feels like pretend compared to the classroom," a boy responds.

"This class doesn't feel all that real, either. I mean think about it for a minute. They pack us together into the smallest space in a building designed like a prison. Maybe phones aren't natural, but neither is this room," a student adds.

"It's not that phones aren't real. It's just a different kind of reality. I wonder if the physical separation actually allows me to listen better . . . or not better, just more intently," another student responds.

I bring up mythology here and it gets dangerous. Not really dangerous. Pretend dangerous. Like war games or fire drills. We talk about the Babel babble of ongoing talk, unceasingly speaking across the globe, promising that we can solve the problems with a higher tower and more cooperation when the tower itself is preventing us to know to one another from our front porches.

We talk about siren calls and the intoxication media promising a relationship while silently dehumanizing us. We get into Prometheus and debate whether or not it is right to steal fire from the gods if it will make life easier.

When it's over, the girl who first claimed telephones were better laments, "I liked this conversation and I feel conflicted. I wish this could have happened with my friends who are outside these walls. Yet I wonder if a telephone can allow for that type of interaction. Do we have to have close proximity to have depth?"

It has me thinking that in our push to be relevant and practical, we miss the larger philosophical dangers of technology. When it is simply about the immediate liability management, educators are less likely to see the long-term dangers. It's like focusing on the need to avoid choking on one's food while ignoring the clogged arteries that will someday lead to a heart attack.

*   *   *

It's Columbus Day, or as Ruth likes to call it Native American Genocide Remembrance Day. If we pack just the right amount of fried chicken, though, we can forget that we live in a land stolen by force and conquest and we can pay attention to the ducks on the pond.

My daughter tosses out leftover pieces of stale bread. I'm pretty sure this isn't the right food for ducks, but it looks cute and I'm feeling restless so I go with it.

Mr. Brown's wife asks me about the telegraph. I explain to her our projects with the telegraph and the telephone. I offer vague answers, assuming that she hears enough from her husband that she probably finds teacher talk to be somewhat dull.

"I like our telegraph, because I can stay connected to my relatives in India," she explains.

"That's the problem," Mr. Brown explains.

"What do you mean?" I explain.

CHAPTER ELEVEN

"At least when you are just in America, you can set your roots in a new culture. But with the telegraph, you live in this strange land in between both places," he laments.

"That's multiculturalism, though. I don't see dual identity as a bad thing," I say.

Mr. Brown adds, "Neither do I. The problem isn't that we are multinational but that we are transnational. The telegraph connects people across the world and ignores the nuances of geography. To me that's a dangerous place to be. We need space," he says.

"Well I like it. Besides, the world has always been transnational because we have always been human. Why can't we unite according to our shared humanity rather than under the name of an arbitrary flag?" Ruth asks.

"I see your point," he adds. "However, technology is a powerful tool and people in power will use those tools to colonize. What did Columbus have? Certainly not moral superiority. No, he had guns and super-bacteria and weapons made of steel. He had some amazing boats that allowed him to connect to the world. And what did he do with those connections? Rape and murder the natives so that we could get a holiday," he says.

Ruth cuts in, "In all fairness, I think he was more about the gold and glory than about a holiday. But I see your point about power."

"That's where it gets confusing for me," I say. "I'm watching the telegraph redefine space and community. I'm watching the pen pal networks change social interaction. I see huge changes as we shift to an image culture. Then, with the telegraph, there's this emerging sense that it's always a sound bite. I often feel conflicted between riding this wave of changing or feeling washed away by the whiplash pace of change."

*   *   *

"How's the phone working?" Mrs. Jackson asks.

"It's working out really well. I mean, there are moments I didn't anticipate. Some kids get scared if they are talking and the room is silent and then others have a hard time hearing if the class is even remotely engaged in task that requires any noise. I hadn't thought of the human side of it."

"That makes sense. But is it a tool you think you will use in the future?" she asks.

"I think so. Here's the thing though: the power isn't in the tool. The power is in the problem solving. See, they're doing a project where they look at an issue in our community. They are looking at themes in their novels, figuring out the problems and actually creating solutions," I explain.

"Very nice, but what happens when they don't create a solution?" she asks.

I get really sarcastic here, "Well, it shows up on the rubric. I have a whole category for it. The boxes are really cute. I made it myself using paper and pencil and . . ."

"No, what happens if there isn't a solution?"

"I'm not sure where you're coming from," I respond.

"What if the solution is a mystery or a paradox? What if it has no solution? Or if the solution causes more damage?" she asks.

"I didn't think about that," I say.

"I just fear that you're beginning with the wrong question. Instead of asking them to explore the problem, you ask them to solve it."

I get really quiet here, feeling ashamed of how excited I had felt just minutes before.

"Tom, by the way, I'm stealing your idea and doing it in my classroom, too. We don't have access to the phone or the telegraph, but we'll use face-to-face interaction instead."

"What about all the questions you just asked me? You sounded pretty critical of the project."

"I'll ask my students the same questions. I want critical thinkers and problem-solvers. I also want students who are humble and recognize complexity and mystery. This is the kind of project where I can bring in both ideas," she says.

*   *   *

One thing that emerges with the student newspaper project is changing our approach to information. They begin to mimic the popular press, where information is instantaneous and chopped up into tiny segments. Mr. Brown says that this is the method of the modern age – that stories are replaced by bulleted points and it strikes me that bullets might just be more dangerous than story.

Who needs a plot when all is action and nothing is noun?

Nouns.

People.

Places.

Things.

Dirt on a bad day.

PENCIL ME IN

Soil on a good day.

Before we moved to Kansas, I used to play in the mud and dig in the cold, hard clay. It was red and wild and on the eve of winter, when death began to creep into our small southwestern town, the sky would turn crimson and we'd be baptized in color.

Trains cut through the land leaving steel spikes. Machinery. Motion. Smoke stack skies of factories and railway stations, baptizing us in soot. On horseback, I can see the land. On train, I can see the whole country and never see the land. We become vapor. John Henry might have won the battle, but the machine wins the war.

I'm supposed to be a progress. I'm supposed to think that things continue moving. But sometimes they don't. Sometimes things just disappear. The modern myth is that the machine will always continue.

I pull out a pencil and it's portable. I never dip it in ink. I never feel the slight variations in the fluid movement of a feather. Cold, hard, mechanical. A neighbor of mine said the pencil is "the best thing since sliced bread." I told him that our family chooses to knead bread together, if nothing else, at least to feel the sticky dough and to toss the flour and to watch the yeast rise slowly. When it is hot, I slice it myself just to remind myself that "the most convenient" doesn't mean "the best."

In the pencil world, we have programs to help my writing flow more smoothly. Nong, Bang, Goggle, Zobo (a whole toolbox with that one - arrives on a train). When I flip through the binder, I used to say "searching through the tabs," but now I just say, "Goggle it," and I wonder if they are like beer goggles - causing me to miss the earthy reality of life.

Eventually, the English language will be reduced to onomatopoeia and all nouns will be verbs and we'll wake up some day a century from now wondering what happened to our sense of space and place and identity.

*   *   *

My wife wrote me a love letter. For Victorian Times, it was pretty steamy. Hell, for any time period it was pretty steamy. She slipped it into my sports coat this morning as I was preparing to ride to work. My horse was sick, so I had to walk. Maybe I just need a mustang. (Or does that require a midlife crisis first?)

So, here's the thing: She wrote it out in pencil. I know it doesn't seem like much, but it bothered me. Pencil is temporary. Pencil is gray. Pencil is movement. Pencil is modern. The graphite letters leave a soot behind that matches the dull gray cloud in this urban landscape, leaving its ugly erasure marks on the ever-changing steel cage neighborhood that I've learned to call home.

Don't get me wrong, I love the letter. It's not the letter itself that bothers me. It's the pencil. It's in this middle zone of being more permanent than speech and more temporary than ink. We say "pencil me in," when we want commitment without commitment. Sometimes it seems as if relationships, community, our most sacred social institutions have of this adopted a "pencil me in" mentality. And that's the problem. The telegraph culture is shaping our relationship in ways that we cannot predict.

PENCIL ME IN

We confuse novelty for innovation and it's all at the cost of long-term public memory. We can't remember anything. No shared stories when they are spliced up into bits and sent via telegraph. No common voice when it's compressed into a phonograph. No flesh and bones when we're extracted and sent across the wire.

So, I walk, with letter in hand, to my factory-styled school, questioning if the pencils are even worth it, wondering if we are penciling in a shady world where nothing is temporary and nothing is permanent. I'm beginning to question life on a graph.

CHAPTER TWELVE
How to Own the World

As part of an award we win for *The Voice Collective*, our students get the chance to go to New York in early April and learn about the technology firsthand. We visit the large brick building of *The World*. At first the name seems to be evidence Pulitzer's hyperbole until we step into the factory where they manufacture public memory.

Our peppy tour guide walks us through the underbelly first, where reams of paper go from pure sheets to disposable information for eager urban consumers.

Eventually we work our way up toward the top, where news begins. Gravel-voiced reporters swap stories with the students, who eagerly share their own experiences with *The Voice Collective*.

"Ooh, I like that name," a reporters mentions. "Has a real Marxist feel to it. Very modern." I don't have the heart to tell him that the student who coined the name *The Voice Collective* probably doesn't know who Marx is.

As we walk away, the peppy tour guide asks, "What do you notice about them?"

"They are all white," a boy mentions.

"They speak English," another student adds.

"They're all men. How will women ever get the right to vote if men control the flow of information?"

"Try not to focus on what they are, but on what they are doing," the guide explains.

Wrong. Focusing on who they are is critical to understanding what they are doing. It's never neutral. Not when you own the world.

*   *   *

We visit Edison's motion picture studio in Manhattan. The students stare at the sleek surroundings and recognize from the decorating alone that this is the sacred place that will eventually write our shared cultural mythology.

As we watch the video production, they are amazed by the magic. Nobody questions the purpose or the meaning or the theme. It's all about the action, the movement, and the motion of the pictures. It isn't real so much as it is an amplified view of reality. Who can compete with a ten-foot tall boxing match?

An Edison representative explains to the students, "We need to prepare students for jobs that don't exist yet."

CHAPTER TWELVE

Preparing students for non-existent jobs? Sounds a bit like training students for jobs in Santa's Workshops.

The representative continues, "We want you to be members of the Innovative Class, where creativity is the bottom line. It's less about knowledge and more about what you do with the knowledge?"

"What does the other class do?" a student asks.

"They work in industry and service," the man responds.

"Oh, we already learned about this in class," another student adds. "It's called Plebeians and Patricians."

A student is visibly upset. He pulls me aside privately. "My mom works and she's smart and creative," he says defiantly.

The man hands me an application to have a motion picture production class within my school. I'm intrigued by the idea of motion picture production.

Motion.

Movement.

Erasing the space and context in our current reality.

Production.

What are we really producing?

The filmmakers chop up bits and pieces of captured, vital life and reproduce it into something new. We're mesmerized by the dancing light and the larger-than-life figures haunting us in their "not-really-here but not-really-gone" sense of permanence. Everything is smoother, grander and more seductive than the terrestrial reality of a schoolyard.

PENCIL ME IN

Yes, I know it is about light hitting a photograph and moving. "Motion picture" sounds tame. But given the nature of light, the paradox of ray and particle, I can't help but see the magic of the motion picture. When they perfect the art of phonography, we'll have talking motion pictures. Perhaps a century from now we'll have it all at the palm of our hands - the ability to pick apart and edit life and present it as something new and magical. We'll have it all available at the push of a button and we'll convince ourselves that we understand it.

*   *   *

"Why can't we get a film studio on campus?" a student asks me.

"I'm not sure about the medium," I tell him.

"So, just teach like you normally would and add some motion picture parts. I bet it would be fun. Imagine what we would produce."

"My goal in teaching has never been to produce fun," I explain.

I disengage for a moment. Something about the Plebeians and Patricians has me thinking of the Roman notion of bread and circus. I always assumed bread was the more powerful element. I'm now understanding the pull of circus. It's not that I am opposed to fun, per se. It's just that often "fun" is the cheap replacement of "intriguing" or "meaningful" or "beautiful" or "life-changing."

"Mr. Johnson, are you okay?" he asks.

"Yeah, I just don't want to create a fun factory," I tell him.

CHAPTER TWELVE

"You know, at the beginning of the year most of us had only used pencils for fun, right? So maybe we use motion pictures to create something that's important instead of fun."

"I wish it were that easy. I wish we could manipulate the medium however we choose. However, it's not that easy. Motion pictures demand fun. They create entertainment. They'll shape the learning in ways that might not be positive," I explain.

"So, what if it's not a positive or negative? What if each tool we use is both good and bad? Do we just throw it out because there are some dangers in it?" he asks.

*   *   *

Educators often believe that they have the power to wield each tool to fit their own purpose. They assume that a lesson can remain virtually unchanged when a new medium is added. Often, the metaphor is one of a tool. However, there is something inherently dangerous about taking every technological device and applying it to learning without ever asking the intended meaning of a medium. A pencil, for example, is inherently individual, deliberately vague, intellectual, portable, and text-based. A film is, by contrast, visual, collective, emotional, and non-linear.

If I begin with a lesson plan and simply pick a tool based upon "fun" or "productivity" or even "student engagement," I am running the risk of teaching something entirely unintended. If I introduce a telegraph as a source of knowledge, we send an implied message that knowledge should be portable, consumable and exist in small increments rather than larger narratives. I am not opposed to adding new tools to learning. I simply want us to recognize that whatever tools we choose will reshape learning in ways that we often fail to recognize.

*   *   *

Later, as we sit down at the restaurant, I'm thinking about *The World* and the telegraph and the motion picture machines. So what does all of that have in common? Colonialism and imperialism.

For all the talk of life-long learning, my school is designed in a factory-meets-prison model of compliance and power and assimilation. On my worst days, I become a prison guard. Some say it is a necessary evil. However, if one considers evil to be necessary, then there is probably a flaw in one's worldview.

I think about the telegraphs and the phonographs sponsored by the robber barons in power. I wrestle with this gift. Is it simply a Trojan Horse? Is it Pandora's box? Is it Prometheus stealing fire from the gods only to let us lose our insides?

I could leave it there and it would be a great rant about robber barons. Except it has me thinking of my own classroom. Technology has layers of social and cultural meaning. Each tool becomes not simply a means of creating, but a means of socialization and potentially indoctrinating. If I have students follow a format, a program of binders, for example, I have imposed my own layer of imperialism and if I'm not careful, I can end up like McKinley and Carnegie and Pulitzer.

The issue isn't simply the technology. The real danger is power. Technology doesn't humanize or dehumanize. Instead, it simply amplifies what is true of humanity, that we are broken and beautiful. If I'm going to be honest with myself, I'm not inherently any better than Pulitzer. It's just that, on my worst days, my audience is smaller, because I have less machinery to amplify my voice. I don't own the world.

CHAPTER THIRTEEN
The World Is Not Flat

I take a seat by the window of the train, my eyes fixated on a monochromatic landscape. The smoke stacks tell the story of a steel steal of all things natural, replacing tradition with movement and space with efficiency. It's the color of a photograph, all value and no color.

I am sitting alone with my pencil, sketching on an iTablet. I'm sketching what I remember of my father. I could capture it better on a photograph, but I'm less in the mood to capture and more in the mood to create. I have this lingering sense that capturing is part of the problem. We are all captive by the monochrome value of industry.

Besides, my whole purpose in sketching is to remember my father for who he was, so that I don't forget him after viewing the casket. Still, I'm distracted. I look out the window. Steel tracks clawing into the tender earth, a tattoo of convenience. It was a Faustian exchange promising instant connections and all the while losing the connection to all that was once sacred – the land, the dirt, community, family.

We will someday wake up with the hangover and convince ourselves that what we really need is a newer fix. We'll grow nostalgic for the railroad, using it for children's stories and decorating devices, while we push forward with newer devices to flatten the world. We already have horseless carriages. Can any horse compete with raw power of a combustible engine?

I imagine that in another half century, we will find a way to fly. We will be Icarus, pushing toward the sun, going further from the ground, detached in a steel-winged cage, stripping away the boundaries of space and time. We'll find ways, no doubt, to extend portability so that even the telegraph seems quaint while the phonograph feels static. Someday we'll have the world at the palm of our hands without questioning whether one should compress the globe so easily. We will find Babel without a blink and we'll marvel not at the power we possess but at the novelty we create.

It's an age of Pi, permanently and randomly marching forward, each step dividing the finite infinitely. We had no need of seconds until we created the railroad. What will we divide next? (Paul thinks we'll divide the atom someday. He says the results will be explosive. I doubt it.)

*   *   *

A man sits next to me. "What do you do for a living?" he asks.

PENCIL ME IN

We begin talking about teaching and I share my vision for my classroom, complete with photographs and a dark room, an area for phonographs, a working telegraph and pencils for every student.

"I want a twentieth century classroom," I explain.

"You can't wait three years for that?" he asks.

"I want a classroom that will be relevant in the industrial age," I respond.

"Oh, like a flat classroom," he says.

"I'm not sure what you mean," I explain.

"One that connects to the world. Columbus proved that the world is round and now we're proving that the world is flat. It's progress. We're being united into a global village."

I'm not about to argue with him on the Columbus point. Just about all of antiquity knew that the world was a sphere. But I'm struck by the word "progress." It is progress, no doubt. Progress in terms of progressing, in terms of novelty and kitsch and pushing toward a climax without questioning the resolution. But it's not progress I'm after right now. It's permanence.

I like the notion of a global village. I like the idea of my students communicating via telegraph and telephone with students across the globe. A part of me really hopes that technology can bridge the barriers of culture and politics and lead to peace. A flat world might just do the trick.

*   *   *

We stop somewhere in Pennsylvania and I sit down at a dingy café for lunch. Sometimes I wish that I could hang a "Do Not

Disturb" sign around my neck and wear it at places where it is socially acceptable to be intrusive. I'd wear it at church, during the "shake hands with each other," time. I'm not so great at sharing the peace. I'd prefer to keep my peace to myself. I'd also wear it when I'm alone with a pencil, trying to work on my Master's work to avoid the thoughts of mortality.

"Is that homework?" a man asks.

"Yes, it's part of my Pencils in Society class," I explain.

"Oh, I see. Is that part of your master's degree?" the guy asks.

"Yes, it is," I add avoiding eye contact.

"Seems like a silly degree to me," he continues.

"I beg your pardon," I finally look up.

"Well, it's just that pencil advocates always complain about not being included in the conversations about education. Yet, they have their own pencil conferences and pencil degrees and pencil plogs. I mean, last time I checked, there was an entire category on the 1896 Eduplogger Awards dedicated to pencil plogs. Don't get me wrong, I use pencils. I should state that outright. I use pencils everyday in my job. Love them. I carry one around with me in my pocket," he explains.

"I'm not sure where you're going with this," I add.

"Well, we don't have a separate world in the workforce that's all about pencils. If I go to a leadership conference, we use pencils. If I go to a workplace productivity conference, we use pencils. But I would never feel the need to get a whole degree in Pencil Business or attend a Business Pencils Conference."

"I see your point. But these venues are necessary as long as we are shut out of the dialogue on curriculum and instruction," I explain.

"As long as educational technology and education remain separate entities, both will exist in a fantasy world of tech-denial or technophilia. See, we'll have all these people gushing about new gadgets in our Brave New Industrial World. We'll hear about connectivity of the telegraph and the global community and all of that and if we're not careful, we'll miss the reality that there are some dark sides to industrialization. Meanwhile, we'll have a separate faction advocating a 'back-to-basics' approach that plays on fear and nostalgia. I'm guessing you're of the technophilia camp, right?"

"I love technology, but I'm no technocrat. My students use paper and pencil, but they also criticize the role of industrialization, the loss of community with technology and the dangers of developing a vapor-self when moving toward a text-based persona," I say.

"I'm glad. We need people who use technology to be focused on the human element first. But here's the thing: wouldn't you be better off introducing technology to people involved in leadership and curriculum and policy?" he asks.

"Perhaps, but there are some big conversations we're having," I say.

"Like what?"

"Like the erasure of geography and what that means for student learning," I respond.

"Oh, like the flat world?" he asks.

"Sure," I say.

"I find that idea really frightening," he says.

"What? We're united. We're a global village. The more global interaction we have, the better the likelihood that we will have peace," I explain.

"I hope you're right. But it seems that the large global economic interests seem like another shot at imperialism. So, great, we have all these alliances. But what if the alliance system works too well?" he asks.

"What do you mean?" I ask.

"It just seems like the world will eventually move into a few big tribes and when those tribes fight, I can't imagine the devastation we'll experience. Imagine a world at war," he says.

"I hold out hope for the flat world," I explain. "We'll finally have peace, actually."

"Oh, and I hope you're right. I just wonder if massive global interaction is always the utopia wish it to be."

"So, you don't think my students should engage with the whole world?" I ask.

"Perhaps they should. But all communication has the potential for conflict and when the barriers are so easily erased, I don't know, it just seems like it can quickly turn into imperialism," he adds.

"I think it's a leveling playing field. It's democracy," I explain.

"Maybe. But if the world is flat, I can't help but wonder if we've been flattened in the process," he says.

PENCIL ME IN

I'm wishing again for my Do Not Disturbed sign. Right now I am definitely disturbed.

*   *   *

Two days later, I am standing on the flat Kansas earth, spade in my hand and tears on my face. It is, in a sense, an escape, if you will, not away from reality, but back to reality. The cool fertile earth calls for a return from where we came. I am burying the dead, refusing to outsource the job to some stranger with no need of closure. Our economy is built on separation of labor, but in this moment, I won't be ruled by economic norms.

The land propels me back into a narrative. I know the people, though I have changed by the flattening, monochromatic forces of industry. I know the story, from exposition to climax and I'm yearning for resolution. I grasp for the theme, having a hunch that it can't be found in a telegraph or a photograph or any other type of graph.

Global village? On a train it sounds so eloquent, but now it's just an oxymoron.

I want my students to use the technology, but I don't want a flat classroom or a flat world or flat learning. Let them learn locally before they go global. Let them know their backyard before they tackle the world. Industry turned my world gray. The trains already etched their name into the ground. When I stand beside my little hometown, I'm not so sure I'm ready for it to be flattened as well.

*   *   *

I share the story of the Flat World and the Global Village with Paul the Preindustrial Poet. I expect him to nod in agreement, but instead he responds with, "Tom, I think you're creating a false dichotomy."

"What do you mean?"

"Why do you have to have either round or flat? Why go global or local? Can't it be both?"

"I'm not sure it can. I think you have to make up your mind where you plant your feet."

"Perhaps. But the forces of a flat world are here regardless of what you feel. If I ignore it, I am doing my students a disservice. I relegate the power to guys like Pulitzer. However, if I teach them to think critically about the whole flat world concept then they can be critical thinking citizens of this flat world."

"But aren't they better off acting in the local community where they at least have a voice?"

"If they only think locally, their world view will be myopic. It becomes tribalism. If they go global without knowing their own backyard, it becomes imperialism and colonialism. If they think globally and locally, they avoid the extremes. They walk in tension, yes, and they face a certain level of confusion. Yet, they also learn to navigate that confusion," Paul points out.

"I see your point, but there is something unnatural about the Global Village," I lament.

"I don't disagree. It's inhuman. It's industrial. We let the steel steal the soul of the people in exchange for instant communication. However, who better to humanize it than your students? Let them act locally and communicate it globally. Let them think about global issues in their own community. But also let them think about how their own locale affects the entire world and if the time is right let them partner across the world with fellow students," he explains.

"That sounds like idealistic romanticism, Paul," I respond.

"I'm not pretending it's easy. I'm not suggesting that pen pal networks will bring world peace. But respectful dialog is a powerful force. And if you don't allow your students to participate in the global dialog you create your own ghetto," he says.

"I guess it's just personal for me. When I was standing on the plains with the sun rising, surrounded by my family, it all felt natural. It felt right. It felt like I lost something when I moved to the city. And it feels like we all lost that something in the process of the flattening of the world," I say.

"You have. We all have. So what do you do next? Have one foot in the factory and one foot on the farm. Have one hand on the pen pal networks and one hand holding a pint with a friend. Garden and write. Be open to the world without shutting out your neighbors. I'm not saying it's easy. Paradox is always harder than polemic pursuits," he explains.

Paul has a point. This is amplified when I arrive home and pick up the pen pal letters. Friends from all over the world (and indeed I now count them as friends) send me their condolences. They engage in meaningful conversation with me in a time when I am raw and vulnerable. I had posted the eulogy to my plog and they wrote some of the most thoughtful things imaginable.

Perhaps a PLN isn't truly a network. Maybe it's a community. Maybe humanity is more powerful than geography. Maybe, as distant as they may be, our letters and telegraph messages patch together relationships that are, indeed, authentic – sometimes more authentic than what is possible in a family too stoic to speak about what's really going on in the heart.

So pencil me in. Don't stain me with ink. Let me live the graphite duality of global and local, of technophile and Luddite of urban and rural. Let me experience the monochrome mystery that never truly hits black and white – the gray reality of paradox. Pencil me in so I avoid the extremes of myopic parochialism and arrogant imperialism. Pencil me in, because life is temporary, a vapor, in constant flux, in tension and harmony.

Pencil me in.

CHAPTER FOURTEEN
Multimedia Masters

A girl stands before a crowd of parents, the projector flickering a fuzzy image of a bird. It sharpens as she begins telling a poem of migration, weaving in and out of metaphors, and a series of seemingly unrelated pictures tying into the story of movement. It's our story. The Gilded Age. The Age of Industry. A time of gray smoke stacks, gray graphite, gray steal trusses and gray trains barreling through our landscape.

She moves to her story, with images of her home and her neighborhood. It's the story of migration as well. She cries when she speaks of learning a new language and no one knows if it's a part of the act or if it's reality. Maybe it's both.

The photography project was part of our larger unit on migration. Mr. Brown and I tied together concepts from math, science, literature and social studies. Though we often read the same texts and engaged in similar dialog, students chose their own project.

One boy compared the movement of a child to the movement of an adult - the migration from free movement as a youngster to the restrictive movement of school on up through the factories, where the machines move and the people are confined to a tiny space. Another student charted the migration of ideas by taking pictures representing various methods of story telling. A girl chose the migration of nature - from the animals to the seasons and the cyclical nature of it.

Some chose to present their projects in a scrapbook. Others chose slideshows. Still, others chose to use SmartCharts. Some integrated painting or drawing into their photography. It wasn't so much differentiated instruction as it was empowered instruction. Students chose not only the concepts but also the media and the presentation methods.

At the end of the presentation, Mr. Brown whispers, "Photographs and phonographs are pretty powerful, huh?"

I answer, "The power was not in the photography or the phonographs or the telegraphs or any of it. The novelty of the medium wore off quickly, with each flashing bulb losing its magical luster. It was replaced, though, with something deeper."

"I know what you mean. I'm getting to where I love technology. However, I love technology, not for the flashing bulbs or the instant access or the efficiency. It has to do with the ability to relate and create and communicate. It has to do with mixing media meaningfully so that learning grows deeper."

My students used text-based resources along with photography. However, the parents were moved to tears in the oldest, perhaps most foreign of all media - the voice, orally spoken, memorized and rehearsed and delivered as if it were the first time. Sometimes a simple tool is what's needed.

$$*\qquad*\qquad*$$

We grab a seat in the balcony, because even at UnConventionAl, the twentieth century un-conference, innovation doesn't include progress in race relations. It's a trend of noticed with some of the techno-utopians who don't want to be bothered with the sticky human issues of social justice. So, as long as Paul remains African-American, we're relegated to the cheap seats.

"We need to cultivate a culture of collaboration to compose a creative class." All alliteration aside, the message is one I've heard repeatedly. I could use the same alliteration if I wanted, "From farms and factories to a philosophy of frenetic futurism."

He pulls out a box and says, "We need to think outside the box." I find it odd that he's using clichés as he talks about innovation. True innovation isn't thinking outside the box. It's re-purposing the box.

"It starts with a pencil and moves to mimeographs and type-writers, photographs and Vitascopes, phonographs and telegraphs. Simple minds and simple tools are fine when you are growing corn . . ." the crowd chuckles. "But you need an innovative mind to think through the mixing and mashing of multimedia tools. Complex tools demand creativity."

My mind races back to cornfields. There is more molecular complexity in an ear of corn than in an entire Vitascope. We lie to ourselves when we think that knowing machinery means we have a deeper, more conceptual understanding of life. Growing up, my family had fewer tools. We had less access to the world at the palm of our hands. But we weren't illiterate hicks. We were a Creative Class.

In my mind now I'm eight, barefoot and staring at a worm. My father is arguing moral philosophy with a neighbor. Dad says that Aristotle had it right - that the goal is a middle ground, a place of temperance between two extremes. The neighbor says the goal is a Hegelian synthesis. Neither men have access to a photograph or a telegraph or a pen pal network. Yet, they are creative thinkers, tackling existential questions from multiple perspectives. It's not flashy, but it's creative.

As their dialog transitions into farming, it becomes a more practical layer of creativity. They are discussing water usage in a time of drought. They converse about sustainability in light of soil erosion and fertilizer. It isn't the tools that lead to their creativity. Instead, they become creative because of limited resources and simple tools.

Farming required more than mere "grunt work," as the speaker describes. (Really, "grunt work?" Were we merely cavemen wandering a sea of corn?) The skill set involved predicting the unpredictable, developing new tools at low costs. Collaboration?

PENCIL ME IN

We had a community co-op that helped us survive. Creativity? My dad could use bailing wire and wood to develop tools that would rival anything Edison is producing.

After sitting through the Creative Class keynote, Paul the Pre-Industrial Poet says to me, "I'm bothered by his message. Tools are great. I don't deny that. It's just that I don't believe that complex tools equal complex thinking."

"It's a bit insulting to those who work blue-collar jobs," I respond.

"I had the same thought. Look, my dad was a slave. We had no tools. We had no power. In fact, to the people in power, we were the tools. But listen to the songs we produced. Listen to the oral history we told. Take a glimpse at the Underground Railroad for a minute. We shaped farming in ways that people will never know. We changed American cuisine. We were a Creative Class as well."

It has me thinking about my class full of multimedia masters. Perhaps there is a time for simplicity. Perhaps creativity doesn't require mastering a ton of new tools.

*   *   *

A few days ago, I gave my daughter a box. She didn't think outside the box. She turned the box into a cave and into a horse and into a home for her doll. I didn't tell her that she had to be creative. She has the creative impulse because she is human.

If I want my students to be creative, I won't tell them to be creative. I won't explain to them that they can be part of the great Creative Class. I'll give them freedom. I'll make learning meaningful. The tools will not "require creativity." Creative thinkers will find the tools and use them in innovative ways.

*   *   *

After leaving the two-day "unconference," Gertrude pulls Mr. Brown and me into her office to attack us for our multimedia unit.

"Mr. Johnson and Mr. Brown, your students never filled out the Migration Packets," she explains.

"No, they created independent projects instead," I explain.

"Yes, I saw. They were cute."

Mr. Brown cuts in, "No, cute is baby bonnets and unicorns. What my students created was powerful."

She continues, "But the Migration Packet was more about problem solving."

I argue, "My students had a migration problem that they solved in groups. It was authentic, connecting ideas of science and social studies and they had to develop a solution . . . "

"Yes, so you solved one problem. The packet had one hundred problems chosen by some of the best educators that Pencil Island could find. We spent good money on learning tools and you neglected them."

"You bought the wrong tools," Mr. Brown replies. "I could build a house, but it would be useless if I bought a stick of dynamite."

I add, "My students went deeper into the content and hit every objective you wanted them to hit. The Pencil Packet was a multiple choice marathon."

PENCIL ME IN

"I see your point, but it is what it is." I hate that phrase. It makes it sound like "what is" cannot change; as if we are reduced to academic fatalism.

She continues, "Tell me, will students answer one question in-depth or do multiple choice on our high-stakes test?"

"Multiple choice," we reply in unison.

"And McKinley's Caravan to the Top is all about test scores, right?"

"But . . ."

"And you agreed to do a common pencil-based unit with the rest of the staff."

Mr. Brown corrects her, "Common is shared. Standardized is imposed. Common is horizontal. Standardized is vertical. I agreed on the objectives that we planned. I never agreed to standardization, though."

"We were creative. The students were creative. And you know what? They learned more in the process," I explain.

"Creative? The curriculum I gave you had tons of tools. You had photography machines, cameras or whatever they're called, so that you could create motivational PowerSlides for your students. Yet, you gave dangerous machines to your students. You essentially let the students become the teachers."

"That's pretty accurate," Mr. Brown responds.

"Well, that's not creative, it's dangerous. Maybe next time you go to the hospital you can ask the other patients to be your doctor," she says.

CHAPTER FIFTEEN
PIE in the Sky

I'm sitting on the front porch, trying to construct a decent plog. My hand wanders toward doodling and I end up sketching fictional characters. It's early summer and I feel like I've lost something now that the school year is over.

I'm yearning for human conversation. Fortunately, my wife comes home and mentions, "We met a wonderful lady at the park. I just felt like I had this connection with her."

"Why is that?"

"I had to correct your daughter," she says, knowing that it irritates me when she says "your" to describe the moments our daughter gets into trouble.

"She had real empathy when I talked about the difficulty involved in having to discipline *your kid*. It turns out one of her sons is E.D. and she feels a stronger sense of guilt every time she gets angry. We talked about authority and authenticity. It was strange to have this great conversation with a total stranger."

"I know what you mean," I say.

"It turns out that she works at your school. Her name is Eunice, I think."

"Really tall, red hair?" I ask.

"Nope. It might be Mildred. Do you have a Mildred?"

"With the big mole on her nose?" she asks.

"No, maybe it's not Mildred. I know, it's Gertrude," she says.

"You mean Gertrude the Enemy of All Things Tom Johnson Wants to Accomplish?"

"That's her?"

"Yep," I say.

"But she seemed so nice. She even talked about how hard it is to do her job when there's so much pressure from above to get the teachers on the same track."

It has me thinking about enemies. Perhaps my wife is right. Gertrude at the Park might be a different person than Gertrude the Destroyer of Plans. Or perhaps she is he same person, but she's as complicated as the rest of us. Maybe she's scared. Maybe she's stressed by dealing with a special needs kid.

Maybe she's human after all.

It has me thinking about the Twentieth Century School proposal. We received the grant and the official permission from the board. It's my chance to build a dream school. I keep telling myself it will be a place that does not dehumanize children and yet I failed all year to see the humanity in our school CANDY LAND specialist.

*   *   *

CHAPTER FIFTEEN

So, I'm at the PIE Conference and I place my slides on the projector. I'm nervous. Shaking. Literally sweating bullets. Okay, not literally, but figuratively. I assure you that there are no flying bullets in my room. I choose the number six, since it's a perfect number and I so badly want something about this presentation to be perfect:

The first slide reads, "Six Lies We Tell Ourselves About Technology." The room is fairly empty, because the topic is impractical. As I start reading the slides, I notice folks on their tablets and notebooks, scribbling pen pal notes to one another. It wouldn't be that difficult, but they keep looking up at the wall, where they set each message. It's called the "back stream," but I'm pretty sure it's the upstream and I'm drowning back stream, watching the novelty of the comments capture their attention. I flip through each slide:

- Lie #1: We can connect to the world and still feel the grass beneath our feet. I tell the story of our neighborhood and the lack of community that exists as a result of newly emerging new transportation, urbanization and the fact that information is now global (thanks to the telegraph)
- Lie #2: What is new is always innovative. I mention that of novelty versus innovation and the fact that often "innovation" is merely hype (I piss a few people off by mocking the iTablet. Note to self: some people love their yellow legal paper, even if it won't let you multitask and take papers out like a real notebook)
- Lie #3: We can control the effects of technology. I mention the changes in Europe after the printing press and how wildlife changed as a result of railroads and barbed wire.
- Lie #4: Quality isn't lost in compression (and the lie that efficiency means effectiveness): Here, I play the mandolin

and then a phonograph and asked them to write down which sounded better.

- Lie #5: Better tools equal better learning. I share the idea that often simpler and fewer tools force students to be more creative).
- Lie #6: It will save time. Time will move on whether we "save" it with gadgets or not.

The workshop is failing miserably. People are drawing pictures and ignoring me. So, I let go and ask, "What are you thinking?"

It becomes a conversation. Slow and awkward at first, but it starts moving.

"I don't think pen pal networks and telegraphs have changed anything," a teacher begins. Folks begin to set their pencils down.

"Me too. If anything, time away forces me to appreciate the grass when I'm back."

"Can't we have it both ways?" another teacher asks.

"I don't think technology makes things better or worse, it just changes things. So, we don't lose our connection to the land. We just view it through a new filter," a teacher explains.

"If we think critically about technology, we can predict its outcomes," someone adds. "We have the control."

Another teacher adds, "Yeah, Tom, you seem to have a pretty fatalistic mentality about things like pencils."

But then another teacher mentions Prometheus and Pandora and quotes a few lines from a Socratic dialog. We talk about the Tower of Babel and the Sirens and the Roman notion of bread and circus. We talk about how often a pen pal letter will pull us away or how the edgy urban environment can make us feel claustrophobic.

CHAPTER FIFTEEN

As we discuss the ideas, I find myself yearning for something low-tech - perhaps a chalkboard where I could be drawing diagrams or taking notes. I feel like a heretic in a high-tech cathedral.

Finally, a teacher says, "I agree with all of these except number two." We discuss it for a while, but I am struck by this notion that our frame of reference for wisdom is anything but innovative. We're going back to Greek and Roman mythology. The teacher, for his part, finally says, "I guess there's nothing new under the sun," quoting a man who lived in an era where the printing press didn't even exist.

Minutes later, we gather around the tables, all hyped up on Coca-Cola. At some point, the conference organizers will realize that a cocaine-laced beverage is probably not the best refreshment before a long-winded workshop on "Pencil Citizenship in the Pencilsphere."

The session begins with an Ice Breaker. A simple glimpse at the hashtags on our pen pal networks would suggest that the ice isn't all that frozen. If anything, we might need a lesson on being kinder in our comments (myself included). But it's the culture of this thing, where quick wit, novelty and sound bytes are more important than story and sustainability.

I'm not sure why we need an icebreaker. We're at a conference, and we're speed dating for acquaintances we'll never see again. It's not that important that I know your trivial background or that you know mine. So, you met Walt Whitman? Nice, but not beneficial to me. So, I once played on a barnstorming baseball team? Again, not that important.

The choice this time is People Bingo. It consists of running around and getting signatures for trivial facts about people's lives. As if Bingo wasn't already the lamest game ever, we have to take away the gambling and turn it into an autograph party. All of a sudden the Wednesday night smoke-field Bingo room just got a lot cooler.

I start envisioning new Ice Breakers. How about Extreme People Bingo, where you have to wrestle people to the ground and get a signature? Or what about turning People Bingo into a drinking game? I've given workshop presentations before and I'll tell you that I wouldn't mind having a slightly liquored-up crowd.

So I go to the pen pal network and write, "Ice-breakers generally fail for two reasons: Extroverts don't need the ice broken and introverts need the ice to melt slowly."

So, it is a waste of time for one group and socially awkward for the other. I take off and wander the conference hall for a bit and then step outside into the cool summer air. Call me icy if you must, but the loud chattering voices are a bit much. Let me hear the breeze.

*   *   *

The next day, I can't access the pen pal networks so I head on over to a smoky breakfast cafe. Apparently the conference didn't anticipate such a high use of paper. So, I'm at a cafe with paper and pencil, plogging my problems. I begin this entry, expecting to write

CHAPTER FIFTEEN

about pencil integration and why it doesn't have to serve economic interests. It needs to be about the human factor instead.

A lady walks in and orders a large coffee. "It's been a tough conference," she begins. "I had two people leave my workshop yesterday and when I checked the pen pal network, one of them had mocked the ice-breaker I developed."

"Oh, that's horrible," the waitress comments. "I know a thing or two about grumpy customers, but none of them have ever left the table mid-meal."

"Do they write 140 character messages that mock you?" the lady asks.

"Nope. Not so much," the waitress responds.

"Couldn't he just have talked to me instead?"

The lady begins crying. She starts talking about missing her husband and her sons and how hard it is to be creative with something like icebreakers when she's not a fan of them in the first place. However, some people like them and so she uses an icebreaker each time she presents.

For the first time, I see her not as a fixture of a conference, but as a human.

I walk up to her and say, "I'm so sorry. I mocked the icebreakers for being artificial and contrived but then I chose the most artificial and contrived method of complaining. It was cruel and insensitive."

The moment is awkward, but she's gracious.

"I'm sorry for crying," she says. "I was stressed."

PENCIL ME IN

"Don't apologize. Your tears are a gift. I needed a change in perspective."

For all the discussions my class had about pencil citizenship last year, I feel like a hypocrite. I failed to understand that even in the transgeographic pen pal world, the bottom line should be humility.

*   *   *

Hours later, the crowd is standing room only as I begin. I'm Icarus soaring up toward the sun. I'm powerful. I'm respected. No spit wads or hunks of paper. Just me, backed up with my PowerSlides set up with the Edison Projector. My previous workshop went over better than I had assumed and now the room is packed.

I offer a give and take, asking critical thinking questions and telling stories. I offer a few bits of humor. It's an easy crowd. People expect safe, campy, cornball humor and so my sardonic, cynical musings seem, if nothing else, like a novelty.

I explain the relationship between social context (the dawn of a Progressive era, urbanization, the rise of industrialization), current educational theory (and its practice) and technology. I mention, as a historical example, the Guttenberg Press meeting the rise of nationalism and the early educational theorist Erasmus. I lock my hands together to show the Triple Convergence and how it is a catalyst for change then move into the notion of collaboration in a New Era.

After talking about a New Pedagogy (which I cleverly refer to as Learning 4.0 just to prove that it is two steps ahead of being 2.0

and all the while feeling, in my gut that I'm still teaching at the Beta level), I offer the question, "as we move forward, what will we do to retain the voice from the past? How will we avoid the pitfalls of perennialism?"

I explain my seven steps and show examples of student work.

Paul the Pre-industrial Poet attends for moral support. I assume that supporting one's morals means boosting one's ego. Wrong. Paul pulls me aside afterward and asks, "Do you really want to know what I thought?"

"Yep. Let me know," I say.

"The slides were great. The points were well spoken. You wowed the crowd with a folksy style meeting with just the right high vocabulary to prove your points. The information was solid, too. I think it got people thinking. But there was one thing missing."

"What's that?" I ask.

"Humility," he says.

"I'm not sure what you're talking about."

"Look, think about the seven steps. These folks have had seven steps and four keys all day long. People are tired, really tired, and all the keys and steps are making them feel like janitors in a packed hotel." He points to the hotel room lobby where style and luxury give an heir of importance to every word. ". . . and they're jumping on all these steps trying to hold onto the heavy key chain and watching the guests having a blast. What are they supposed to do with all this?"

"So, what would you have done differently?" I ask.

PENCIL ME IN

"Okay, you know how you say pencils are not the magic bullet? You just presented them as the magic bullet. You showed the best student examples and told the most enlightening stories. You advertised yourself and although the crowd felt entertained, where do they go from there? Do they visit a fantasy land? Tell some stories of failure. Tell a story of a snapped pencil or a paper glider. Show a time when a student failed to get it and ask the crowd for advice. They might not be pencil geeks, but they are experts in some area," he tells me.

Paul is right. So if I'm Icarus, I'm crashing toward the ground. I'll be greeted with adoration from those who attended the workshop. We might talk theoretical nonsense and I might move closer to the sun. Or maybe I can stop pretending that I'm cutting edge and admit that the edge has cut me up pretty badly in the process. I think about Gertrude for a moment as well. I'm pretty sure she's still removing some of the shrapnel from the Icarus explosion.

I look around at the conference environment. We're creating a PIE in the sky and we're not grounded. We're not humble. We're not honest about the fact that teaching is a really hard gig and no amount of techie tools will fix that.

I have one more workshop to lead. Maybe I'll just be what I am - a guy who is lost in a quickly changing industrial world, a little scared and lonely and confused by the fact that I cannot see the stars. Maybe I'll tell a few stories of failure and engage in a conversation about being relevant without selling out.

CHAPTER SIXTEEN
Steam Punk or Sellout?

So, the grant went through and they're now our school is becoming a Twentieth Century School. Note the proper noun. It's very proper. We finally matter.

Part of implementing the new school concept involves switching from a full-time teaching position to that of an Pencil-Integrated Specialist position.

"I'm afraid I'll lose perspective. I'll forget what the classroom is like," I tell Ruth.

"You'll be fine," she reassures me. "You get to coach."

"Not really," I lament. "I don't get to blow whistles and yell at people."

"Good coaches have never been good yellers," she says.

PENCIL ME IN

"You know, I'm still bothered by the funding of it. I once protested at one of Carnegie's factories and I'm nervous about robber barons that try and buy influence. I'm nervous that their voice will win out and that we'll move toward job skills instead of learning to live well. I'm worried about the factory model of education. We say that this is progressive, but moving forward doesn't always mean moving up," I say.

"I know. We've had these conversations. If you can remember the human element, you'll be fine," she adds. "Besides, can't you offer that perspective? You can be the one to steer the program that direction."

*   *   *

It's five o'clock and Meat the Teacher night is beginning. The crowd is extra large due to the issues with an error in homophones (or homonyms - I can't always keep them straight), assuming that the teachers were putting on a barbecue, which would be cool because nothing builds community like the collective bonds of setting animal flesh on an open flame and then digging into the carcass while talking about the weather.

A man pulls me aside and introduces me to his son. "You'll like his class, Josiah." One of the perks of this coaching gig is that I am allowed to teach one period of journalism a day.

He then whispers to me, "He's a Graphite Geek. Plays Hang Man and other violent paper games non-stop. He loves pencils. I'm guessing he'll love your class."

I whisper back, "I hope he likes learning, because we don't really play Hang Man in my class."

CHAPTER SIXTEEN

I sigh, realizing that this will be another year of reminding students at the beginning that the pencils are tools, not toys.

The principal strolls into my room. "How did my speller check not catch that?" he asks.

"It's not misspelled. It's misused," I explain.

"What's the point of technology if it's going to fail on you?" he asks.

"Yeah, it can be unpredictable," I say.

"Must be a glitch," he adds.

The dictionary didn't fail him. The failure was human. Technology is predictable and flawless, making mistakes only when programmed improperly. The beauty of humanity is that we aren't predictable, because as hard as the district office tries, we can't be programmed. It's why we can be creative. It's why we have stories. We're not mechanical. Nothing is clockwork.

The principal humbly faces the consequences by running across the street to the meat market. Gertrude rounds up a few parents to bail him out and spread the news that it's a "bring your own meat" barbecue. It's that rare moment when a micromanager saves the day.

Around six thirty we're all eating. A pick-up game of baseball has started among the parents. The kids, losing interest, have started their own game in the street. I end up playing soccer with a few of my future students. It strikes me that this is how it should always start, not with lectures and rules and procedures, but by playing together. None of us say anything, but they are seeing who I am as a person so that they can understand who I am as a teacher.

PENCIL ME IN

We've gone from an awkward "meet and greet" to an all-out carnival - united by the shared celebration of learning and the shared experience of burning animal flesh. What I fail to see is that this applies to our Twentieth Century School as well. If it's going to be real, if it's going to work, if it's going to last, it's going to be human and it's going to include conflict and mistakes.

*   *   *

Within the first week of the Twentieth Century School implementation, a group of teachers come to me with their concerns about a lack of decent pencil skills. I hadn't predicted this. Students are snapping pencils and saying they just don't know how to use them. Others have turned papers into projectiles. Still others have turned to playing violent games of Hang Man.

"I had two students forget to save their documents," a teacher mentions.

"Could that be an issue of their age rather than a pencil skill? I mean, a hundred years from now we'll probably still have students who forget to put their names on their papers." I ask.

"It wasn't an issue with slates," the teacher responds.

"Yes, but you didn't have to write names on slates," I say.

"Another one couldn't figure out how to put his documents in a folder. I have others who just leave every document on the desktop. Aren't they supposed to be Pencil Natives?"

"I heard that's just a myth," another teacher adds. "Turns out the 'Pencil Native' generation aren't all that technologically savvy at all. It's just hype created by pencil pushers hell bent on ruining slate-based learning." I know the study she's referring to and it seems to prove little more than what I already experience: students still have gaps in their ability to use pencils in meaningful ways.

The gripe fest continues until I ask the teacher, "What is their native language?"

"English," a teacher adds. "Some of them Italian and German, but mostly English."

"And do you still have to teach them grammar and spelling?" I ask.

"Yeah," the teacher says.

"You don't say? You mean they don't pop out of the womb diagramming sentences?" I ask.

"No, but . . ." the teacher protests.

"And what is their native country?" I ask.

"Most of them are from here," the teacher says.

"Do we still teach civics? I mean, if they are American, they should come out of the womb knowing all about democracy and the bicameral legislature and the writ of habeas corpus," I say.

"Oh no, we still have to teach them that," the teacher says.

"Could it be that one's status as a native has more to do with comfort, culture and values and less to do with skills? When I look at my students, they are comfortable with pencils. They identity with the modernist, sketchy-gray worldview. They understand conceptually the notion of portable information via the telegraph and telephone. It doesn't mean they are information engineers with perfect penmanship, however."

*   *   *

PENCIL ME IN

Later that week, a teacher says to me, "Hey Techno-Tommy, when you're on prep I need you to come by and sharpen my pencils." She turns to another teacher and says, "I know he loves working with pencils."

Wrong. I love to write with pencils, because I love words. I love to draw with pencils, because I love creativity. I take good care of my pencils, not because I have a special affinity for pencils, but because they are my tools. It's called stewardship.

What I want to say is, "Sorry, but you need to figure out how to use the sharpener. I know it looks dangerous and it's made out of metal, but I assure you that you can figure it out. I'll walk you through it the first time and then you do it on your own the next time. You have to run an update on each pencil and keep them sharp or eventually they won't work. It's a simple crank. You can do it!"

Our custodian walks by and points out to me, "You know, last time I checked, I had to learn how to take care of my tools. I had never used a tape measure before. Seriously, I just eyeballed it. So, when they gave me a tape measure, I didn't find a measure man and ask him every day how to roll the tape back up. I learned it, because I knew I needed to know how to use it if I wanted to keep my job."

"I'm guessing you could figure out how to use a pencil sharpener, too," I respond.

"I do. You crank that fu-"

"Please, these are Victorian times. Let's keep our language clean," I remind him.

"But you see what I mean. I wouldn't break a pencil and say 'well that's not my thing.' I wouldn't tell the people in charge that it's 'not in my job description' to learn how to use a sharpener. After all, these people have to shake out the chalk dust from their erasers, don't they? It's a part of the job. You learn to use and take care of your tools."

"Some people are scared. I get that, I really do. Ask me to work on a horseless carriage and I'd be terrified. So, on some level, I understand how the teachers feel about pencils. Plus, they are rushed for time. It can feel like one more demand," I remind him.

"If that were me, I'd find a kid who is comfortable with pencils and I'd have him teach the class how to sharpen their own pencils. I'd learn a skill, a student would be able to teach others and we'd all save time. Then again, I'm just a janitor." I wonder what would happen if more teachers had the mindset of a custodian.

As I leave, a teacher says to me, "Hey Techno-Tommy, I need you to fix this paper. It seems I can't erase it for some reason."

"It's covered in scribbles. Have you considered updating your paper and using a new page?"

"Just make it work," he tells me.

The same morning, as I'm setting up for lesson plans, another teacher walks in. "My notebook is broken."

"What do you mean, broken?" I ask.

"The rings won't work anymore," she explains. "I have no idea what happened." This is code word for, "I dropped this and don't want to buy a new binder."

Another teacher says, "My paper is broken."

PENCIL ME IN

"What do you mean 'broken?' Is it ripped?"

"No, it just looks all gray and there are some holes in it."

"Did you update it at all?"

"You mean, they expect me to run updates on this! I thought paper was supposed to be easier than slates."

*   *   *

"I get the sense that they are all trying to sabotage the plan," I tell Paul.

"Are you sure it's sabotage?" his wife, Gloria, asks.

"Come on, they can use a sharpener. They're not stupid. It's just that they don't like being told they have to use new tools," I say.

"Maybe that's the problem. Maybe they aren't experiencing freedom," Gloria adds.

"Or maybe they really did expect technology to fix all problems," Ruth adds.

"I can't see where they would have gotten that idea," I mention.

Paul looks at me and says, "Tom, I read your proposal. The teachers read it, too. You mentioned all the benefits of technology but never mentioned the costs."

Ruth looks at me and says, "You really did sell it to them. Maybe they feel like it's a bait and switch."

"I see what you're getting at, but they need to learn. If they're halfway decent at teaching, they can figure out paper and pencil," I say.

CHAPTER SIXTEEN

"It's a slow process, Tom. Let it happen organically," Paul explains. "Besides, you need to coach them. You need to draw it out of them. When you come at them like an enemy, they're going to respond like that. Just remember your own frustration at the beginning of your own pencil process."

*   *   *

I decide to revisit the Place with Pencils, where pencil integration had been meaningful and the teachers worked as co-researchers. My glossy-eyed edu-crush is shattered, however, when I meet with the principal.

"I'm amazed with what you have at your school. How did you pull it off?" I ask.

"Tom, this place got real political when we began to change. Twelve teachers quit. They were good teachers, too. One of them left the profession altogether telling me that if he wanted to work for a corporation he would go into business. People want autonomy and we were asking people to reject practices that weren't working. One teacher told me that she relished in being the Worksheet Warrior. This place works because the teachers agree upon this model. But we also ran some good practices into the ground that first year. We told a teacher he had to replace his debates and philosophical discussions with pen pal styled forums and shared documents. We were too forceful at first," he explains.

"I'm impressed by the way it runs," I tell him.

"Sometimes I worry that we simply attracted great teachers and then some of them have had their hands tied in collaboration and might be more effective if left alone," he says.

"It seems like it's working, though," I respond.

"Maybe so, but change doesn't happen in a vacuum. The social and political and economic forces are hard. You know for a fact that both political parties have been involved in handing out administrative jobs, right? And the large textbook companies essentially bribed our Governing Board. I almost lost my job in the first year," he explains.

"So what does that mean for my school?" I ask.

"What I'm saying is to avoid the thoughts about reform. If you want to be effective, teach well. Focus on your group of thirty students. If you are using pencils and paper effectively, it will catch on. The change will happen organically. Mentor the teachers who want help. They'll be the early adopters and it will spread," he says.

"But your school created structures for change. Your teachers do research and plan curriculum together and . . ."

"I know, but sometimes I wonder if they would have been better off without so much rigid structure. What's important is that they're talking about instruction instead of arguing about discipline or complaining about parents. Besides, things didn't improve for us until I backed down a bit and gave them the reins. For example, the whole teacher-as-researcher came from the staff and even then, we have a few teams who rejected that model," he explains.

"So you had to move away from your plan?" I ask.

"Nothing looks like it did in our original plan. Nothing. The structural changed you mentioned happened from the ground up. The teachers began to change things."

*   *   *

CHAPTER SIXTEEN

A week later, I'm in the library beginning my PowerSlide presentation entitled "The Teacher-Researcher: A Vision for the Twentieth Century." I begin my sales pitch, "We went from one room school houses to a cluster of one room school houses. What we need is a professional place. We need teachers working together scientifically sharing their research."

Heads nod in agreement. A few teachers grow antsy, because I'm deliberately avoiding the Buzzword Bingo words.

My own words "school houses" echo in my brain.

Schoolhouse.

I'm back in my childhood. Our one-room schoolhouse was just that - a house, a second home of sorts. We sat together and learned together, with the older students mentoring the younger ones. Our teacher was not a professional. He was like a second father to me. Call it paternalistic. Call it parochial. Call it small and narrow-minded, but my mind expanded in that narrow context.

The schoolhouse was an extension of the community. It wasn't created to mimic a factory or an office or any other economic institution. It wasn't meant to "prepare students for the technological advances so desperately needed in an industrial age." It was a social institution that belonged to the community.

Silence.

I can't speak.

Memories of dirt and bare feet and the smell of manure on the flat plain. It's not nostalgic so much as real. Vivid not in the imagination, but in that very terrestrial reality – under the pavement of the factory school. It's the dirt under the fingernails. I don't know what a twentieth century student needs, but I know what we all want: authenticity.

Throw a seed.

Water it.

Watch it grow.

Or not.

Change is always a mystery. Progress is paradox. Who am I to tell you how to teach? Go figure it out. If you like what I'm doing, adopt it as your own.

The staff murmurs in the midst of my silence. They rustle papers and pass notes.

"What I'm saying is all wrong. All wrong." It's awkward. The flickering bulb of the Edison projector keeps pace for me, quietly reminding me of the marching of machinery, but I can't talk.

I turn off the projector. A small act of liberation, not against the forces of technology, but against something else – perhaps the propaganda plan forged by a man who desperately wanted to move the school forward without ever asking if forward was better. I kept saying that what I wanted was a 20th Century Education. Not true. I wanted to be the expert. I wanted to be innovative. I wanted to be important in a world where I can all-too-often feel penciled in.

"It's not that I'm against technology. I just . . ." I stammer slowly, "I just don't know. I'm not the expert. I know what works for me with my students in my classroom. And I'd like a conversation about pencils and telegraphs and whatnot. But I haven't allowed for a conversation. It's been one-sided."

CHAPTER SIXTEEN

The staff is silent. I finally have their attention. They're growing closer to me.

"Do you ever miss the one room schoolhouse?" I ask.

"Nope," a teacher begins. "My teacher was mean. He would paddle you if you asked the wrong questions."

"I miss it. I miss how we used to learn with people at different ages."

We begin a brainstorm: a connection to the local community, a connection to the land, multi-age learning opportunities, mentoring and apprenticeships, school as a civic rather than economic institution and a connection to classical learning. Slides and telegraphs are great, but so is Aristotle, the teacher as a leader rather than a cog in an educational factory.

It begins to make sense to me. I went from railing against the factory to trying to create a different kind of factory. Collaboration was okay as long as it fit my vision of education. I tried to bribe teachers with new tools. I offered it as a fix-all. Now, they are resentful of their lack of freedom and the false promises I had made. They need the autonomy of the schoolhouse.

"This is going to be a messy process," I warn them. "It won't happen easily. We all have a story. We're all on a journey. Some of you are just falling in love with pencils. Some are advanced. Some are skeptics. And you know what? That's okay. We'll do this journey together at our own pace," I say.

I scan the room. Not a single teacher is holding a Buzzword Bingo card.

*   *   *

PENCIL ME IN

A pencil is temporal. The lines of fluid, sketchy, shades of gray blended softly. Mistakes are erased, words rewritten. Nothing lasts. The medium demands a rewriting. Movement toward mastery. It's the myth that if we keep rewriting, we might reach perfection.

What does this mean that truth cannot simply be crossed out, but erased and rewritten? Books may not be burned, but simply altered subtly.

Fluid gestures.

Movement.

Space.

Erasures of all things permanent.

I stand barefoot in the backyard, bathing in the moonlight, wondering if there is any place left to stand. On some level, I welcome the movement. I relish in the connections. I have never been rigid. Let my hands smudge in the shades of gray rather than stained in black and white. But I yearn for permanence. I yearn for geography. I yearn to be off the grid and off the graph.

But I also yearn to be in the moment, in the temporary, in the movement and the progression. I yearn to believe that change can be good and it can grow and it can be sustainable. I yearn for the ambiguity and the paradox of gray.

I step one foot on the pavement, an overly dramatic gesture in a solitary moment when no one can laugh at my one-person object lesson. I squat down to see the cracks and the crab grass inching forward slowly. Perhaps the tortoise will win in the end. Call it a contradiction or a paradox, perhaps even both. But I won't walk away from the industrial, technological pavement. I want to see something real and sustainable and authentic growing out of it. Don't fix the concrete with a newer, better layer. Plant a seed and let it grow underground.

*   *   *

My wife and daughter are asleep. I wander away for a while. We live near a factory and a high-rise apartment complex. I hear laughter and whistling and shouting from neighbors who never seem to sleep. It sounds too melodramatic, too cliché and too stereotypical. I want them to sound more creative and profound and philosophical.

I stand by the factory. The smokehouse is beautiful. It shouldn't be. I know it's dangerous. But the clouds seem to dance to the steamy song of industry illuminated by the ancient rays of a medium that changes by the night. Someday people will miss the smokestack. It will first be obsolete and then nostalgia will kick in and the factory will feel vintage.

The lie of the technocrats is that we can create something better simply because we can create something newer. It's not the lie of "them." It's my own lie. It's the lie I tell on the pen pal network when I mock ice breakers and the lie I tell when I present before a packed crowd and the lie I told, straight-faced, to the robber barons who wanted a crack at our students' skulls. It's the lie of Icarus – that going further and higher and faster automatically means better.

There is an opposite lie; that of the Luddites. It's the lie that the past was better, that the technology tools were less corrupt, that new technology simply dehumanizes when it is always both, unpredictably changing and shaping the human race. It's my own lie as well, when I get really self-righteous with people about our lack of electricity in our home and why horses trump automobiles.

If there is something missing from both sides of the techno-debate, it is the concept of humility. It's the same thing that was missing from my PIE Conference talk. It's what was missing from my 20th Century Grant proposal. It's what was missing from my approach with Gertrude and on my worst days, it's what's missing in my classroom.

I think back to the kid on the fire escape and the sketchpad and the poetry. What made the pencil powerful was that it was in my hands. It was personalized. I had autonomy. I had power. And yet, it was humble. Maybe that's ultimately where pencil integration needs to lead us.

I pull out my sketchbook and start to draw the smokestacks. I want to capture the beauty of imperfection. No "capture" is the wrong word. I want to reflect the reality that we are beautiful and broken in our gray industrial existence.

RECOMMENDED PLOGS

Tom Johnson's Edublog Award Nominations 1897

Here's my list:

- Best Individual Plog: This was a hard one, but I'm having to go with *Waldo's Pond*. I love the way he takes up Thoreau's notion of finding a pond and thinking about life. The combination of poetry, sketches and thoughtful reflection make this a truly literary education plog.
- Best Individual Tweaker: With the explosion of opium dens and the use of cocaine in medicine, I'm a bit shocked that anyone would ever glorify the concept of a tweaker. Shame on you, Eduplog!
- Best Group Plog: Caravan to the Valley does a great job creating a satirical plog mocking William McKinley's Caravan to the Top.
- Best New Plog: Theodore Grant's Losing My Sideburns deals not only with what it's like to be a new teacher who must shave his sideburns and dress professionally, but also what it means to completely lose one's former identity in becoming the "man in charge" at this one room schoolhouse.
- Best Class Plog: I'm Down with Brown. It's a brilliant plog dealing with social class issues in the southwest. Topics such as marginalization and racist language (hence the brown).
- Best Resource Sharing Plog: 20th Century Learning Resources - George has a way of finding all the resources that are necessary for the Industrial Age and locating them in a daily paper. Nice work, George! Where else will I find the 18 Ways to Integrate Origami into Daily Paper-Based Instruction?
- Most influential Plog Post: We Are the Factory. I love the notion that in creating this current modern factory model, those of us who are complicit in it become the factory itself.
- Most influential tweet / series of tweets / tweet based discussion: I almost went with the meadowlark on this one, but I'd have to say the robins at Steele Park. Seriously, some amazing tweets going on there. Just listen. Set your tablet down and listen to the music. Oh, oh, oh, listen to the music. All the time.
- Best Teacher Plog: Learn to Serve. I love the way Ruth gets her children

to serve without feeling coerced or falling into the overly progressive trap of "let's go fix the world."

- Best Librarian / Library Plog: Mary Emerson's Damn Dewey's Delightful Decimal System is a mildly irreverent description of the life of a lonely librarian with a keen sense of alliteration and irony.
- Best School Administrator Plog: *I Assist in Intending, in a Super Kind of Way* is an honest, funny and often bizarre portrait of an assistant superintendent of a small rural district.
- Best Educational Tech Support Plog: A Sketchy Solution has saved me on many occasions when I simply couldn't figure out how to fix a pencil.
- Best eLearning / Corporate Education Plog: *Thomas Edison's Education Funhouse* might be a bit overly corporate, but come on, it's Thomas Effing Edison, guys! The man who invented (or had other people working for him who invented) the light bulb - the very symbol we will forever use when drawing clip art pictures of people with an idea. If we're going to have corporate buyout of education, let's at least keep it entertaining in the process.
- Best Educational Use of a Phonograph: *Can You Hear Me Noun?* is genius in the way it captures both the limitations and the strengths of the phonograph and the human voice in education and grammar in particular.
- Best Educational Use of Motion Pictures: *Check Out Some Skin!* I realize the marketing on this one failed, with many patrons assuming it would be a peep show. But regardless of the box office dud, this was a real hit with my classroom. Who knew the epidermis could be so fascinating?
- Best Educational PowerSlide: *How PowerSlides Lost Their Power* is a self-mocking PowerSlide making use of everything we dread when we hear the first rumbling of that Edison projector: comical typeface, cheap stock photography, entire paragraphs on one slide. You get the idea. Genius satire, in my opinion.
- Best Educational Use of a Social Network: Ray's Cafe. Just go there sometime and try the pie or the pi. Either way, you'll never have enough. People connect in a deep social network on a daily basis.
- Best Educational Use of a Virtual World: Isn't that precisely schooling already is? A dark virtual world with draconian discipline all in the name of the "real world?"

ABOUT THE AUTHOR

E-mail: socialvoice@gmail.com
Blogs: johntspencer.com and educationrethink.com
Twitter: @johntspencer

John T. Spencer has taught social studies, computers and self-contained seventh and eighth grade in Phoenix, Arizona (where he enjoys spending time with his wife and three children). He has experience in leading professional development and developing a technology-integrated curriculum.

Made in the USA
San Bernardino, CA
01 May 2013